M000074820

By Dawn's Early Light

Donna-Marie Cooper O'Boyle

By Dawn's Early Light

———— ☆ ————

Prayers and Meditations
for Catholic Military Wives

SOPHIA INSTITUTE PRESS
Manchester, New Hampshire

Sophia Institute Press
Box 5284, Manchester, NH 03108
1-800-888-9344

www.SophiaInstitute.com

Sophia Institute Press® is a registered trademark of Sophia Institute.

Library of Congress Cataloging-in-Publication Data
Names: O'Boyle, Donna-Marie Cooper, author.
Title: By dawn's early light : a prayer book for women in the service and
   military wives / Donna-Marie Cooper O'Boyle.
Description: Manchester, New Hampshire : Sophia Institute Press, 2018. |
   Includes bibliographical references.
Identifiers: LCCN 2017053958 | ISBN 9781622824748 (pbk. : alk. paper)
Subjects: LCSH: Catholic women—Prayers and devotions. | Women and the
   military. | Women soldiers—Prayers and devotions. | Military
   spouses—Prayers and devotions.
Classification: LCC BX2170.W7 O255 2017 | DDC 242/.88—dc23 LC record available at https://lccn.loc.gov/2017053958

First printing

For my children, Justin, Chaldea, Jessica, Joseph, and Mary-Catherine, and my grandchildren Shepherd James and Leo Arthur; and for my father, Eugene Joseph Cooper, who served in the National Guard.

Also for my brothers Gary John Cooper and Timothy John Cooper, who served in the Vietnam War, and to all the heroic military men and women who have come before us and all those who will continue to serve.

May God bless one and all!

Contents

Part 3

Prayers for Every Occasion

By Dawn's Early Light

Introduction

If you want peace, work for justice.
If you want justice, defend life.
If you want life, embrace the truth:
the truth revealed by God.

— St. John Paul II, homily, January 27, 1999

This book is for all women associated with the military, whether on land, on sea, or in the air—those married to men in the military; mothers, daughters, sisters, aunts, nieces, or cousins of soldiers; and all those at home who are waiting for their loved ones to return or who are living on military bases, or struggling with the myriad demands connected with military life.

This book is for you.

I witnessed my mother's tears on many occasions when my brothers Gary and Tim were on the other side of the world fighting in Vietnamese jungles. There's no doubt about it. War is ugly. War changes us. It takes away our loved ones—sometimes for a time, while they are deployed, and in other cases, forever. As a young girl, I worried so much about my older brothers when they were fighting in the Vietnam War. I thought I might not be fortunate enough to see both come home alive. I knelt beside my bed every night, pleading with God to keep them safe: *Please bring them home, dear Lord!* Thankfully, they both came back. But they were no doubt changed for having been there. Gary has since passed on to his eternal reward due to cancer that might have been linked to his exposure to chemical weapons.

War is ugly indeed, but those who engage in battle to protect innocent human life are amazingly beautiful heroic souls. G. K. Chesterton once said, "The true soldier fights not because he hates what is in front of him, but because he loves what is behind him."[1] For some time now, I have felt inspired to write a book for military women. Ever since I was invited to speak to the women at West Point several years ago, I felt a special connection with them and wanted to write a prayer book for them. In fact, I told the lovely ladies that very night that I would write a book for them. Later, I was invited to speak to a couple of groups of military women at Fort Bliss, Texas, and after that I was a keynote speaker at the Worldwide Conference of the Military Council of Catholic Women (MCCW) in Washington, D.C. My heart goes out to these gallant women, and I am overjoyed and blessed that they have "adopted" me as an honorary lifetime member of their worldwide community and have asked me to speak at their conference again.

Military women are very special "soul sisters." They share a certain military pride; they are in solidarity in their goal to defend human life, to fight injustice, and to protect their country. They have heroically placed their lives on the line on battlefields as well as in battling military issues on the home front, dealing with the devastation of war and how it has encroached upon their families, battling the stress of numerous moves and transitions, intense worry, uncertainty, post-traumatic stress disorder, depression, anxiety, alcoholism, suicide, and much more that comes with the territory.

I want to tell their stories: their heartaches, their pains, and their amazing triumphs. I want to shine a light on them — to give honor and praise to these deserving women who carry on with humility, albeit at times feeling as if they are groping in the dark at what lies ahead, while clinging tenaciously to the gift of faith growing in their hearts and souls. Their heroism

---

[1] G.K. Chesterton, *The Illustrated London Times.*

doesn't remain on the battlefield; it's woven into the very fabric of their lives.

In addition, I also deeply desire to offer prayers and inspiration that will give them a powerful shot in the arm, to uplift their spirits and encourage them to put one foot in front of the other to continue to walk in faith.

When I think of faithful and prayerful women working together or helping one another, I cannot help but ponder our Blessed Mother and particularly her visit to her older cousin St. Elizabeth. Immediately after the angel Gabriel appeared to Mary at the Annunciation to inform her that she was going to be the Mother of God, before Mary even took time to ponder the whole idea of suddenly becoming pregnant after being overshadowed by the Holy Spirit, the beautiful virtue of charity moved her to proceed "in haste" to the hill country to be of service to her cousin who was also pregnant, but late in life. Mary didn't worry about her own pregnancy discomforts or even about what St. Joseph might say when he would see her protruding baby bump three months later upon her return. She simply and deliberately put her needs aside and set out on a faithful pilgrimage to help. After all, she was, as she called herself, "a handmaid of the Lord" (Luke 1:38). We can imagine that Mary was a tremendous help to Elizabeth and that Elizabeth was a great comfort and steady source of seasoned holy wisdom for Mary. May we women strive to imitate their holy, virtuous lives.

I feel blessed to write these words on the feast of the Visitation of the Blessed Virgin Mary. I pray that this book will speak to the hearts of military mothers, grandmothers, stepmothers, godmothers, wives, aunts, sisters, cousins, nieces, and all women who are serving or have served in the military. I hope that this book will also be a constant source of prayer and inspiration for anyone who is connected to the military, as well as the patriotic, and anyone who would like to learn more about these courageous military women. I pray that God will bless each and every one in great abundance!

I still carry the very worn wooden rosary that a kind chaplain at West Point gave me, and I have prayed with it all these years since. I will continue to pray for the military and their families. I hope you will join me.

Yours in prayer and the love of the Holy Family,

Donna-Marie Cooper O'Boyle

May 31, 2017

Visitation of the Blessed Virgin Mary

Part 1

True Stories of Active Service

Sergeants are proverbially believed to be hard and tough.
It is not likely that they were any different on Calvary.
It was a Roman sergeant, so used to scenes of blood,
who ran a spear into the side of Christ.
But he was converted on the battlefield,
and in that very hour he declared his faith:
"Indeed, this is the Son of God."
Maybe I can find Christ on the battlefield, too.

—Servant of God Fulton J. Sheen, *Wartime Prayer Book*

1

The Perfect Woman

For all that is in the world—the desire of the flesh, the desire of the eyes, the pride in riches—comes not from the Father but from the world. And the world and its desire are passing away, but those who do the will of God live forever.

—1 John 2:16–18

No woman is perfect ... well, except for the Blessed Mother! Take that pressure off your shoulders right now. We will discuss the crazy demands for perfection that women face. But first, let's get to a few prayers to get us headed in the right direction!

Prayer is essential to our spiritual health and well-being. We couldn't survive without it. St. Thérèse of Lisieux said, "For me, prayer is a surge of the heart; it is a simple look towards heaven; it is a cry of recognition and of love, embracing both trial and joy."[2]

I find that praying a Morning Offering when I open my eyes to face a new day starts that day off with the right disposition. Through a Morning Offering, we hand the reins over to God. We trust that He will guide us throughout the day and that He will transform its challenges and sufferings into valuable graces for our souls and those of others when we lovingly offer them all to Him for His glory. We pray that His holy will may be accomplished through us. And, when things suddenly turn chaotic, we can pause to recall that we gave it all to our loving Lord at the beginning of our day. He has this! He will help us. We can turn to Him again in that moment and pray for His grace.

---

[2] St. Thérèse of Lisieux, *Manuscrits autobiographiques*, C 25r, quoted in the *Catechism of the Catholic Church* (CCC), no. 2558.

By Dawn's Early Light

Morning Offering

O Jesus,
through the Immaculate Heart of Mary,
I offer You my prayers, works,
joys, and sufferings of this day
for all the intentions of Your Sacred Heart,
in union with the Holy Sacrifice of the Mass
throughout the world, in reparation for my sins,
for the intentions of all my relatives and friends,
and in particular for the intentions
of the Holy Father. Amen.

A Morning Prayer

St. Thérèse of Lisieux (1873–1897)

O my God!
I offer Thee all my actions of this day
for the intentions and for the glory
of the Sacred Heart of Jesus.

I desire to sanctify every beat of my heart,
my every thought, my simplest works,
by uniting them to Its infinite merits;
and I wish to make reparation for my sins
by casting them into the furnace
of Its merciful love.

The Perfect Woman

O my God!
I ask of Thee for myself
and for those whom I hold dear,
the grace to fulfill perfectly Thy Holy Will,
to accept for love of Thee
the joys and sorrows of this passing life,
so that we may one day
be united together in Heaven
for all eternity. Amen.

Prayer of Dedication for Morning or Evening

Lord Jesus,
I give You my hands to do Your work.
I give You my feet to go Your way.
I give You my tongue to speak Your words.
I give You my mind that You may think in me.
I give You my spirit that You may pray in me.

Above all, I give You my heart that You may
love in me your Father and all mankind.

I give You my whole self
that You may grow in me,
so that it is You, Lord Jesus,
who live and work and pray in me. Amen.

By Dawn's Early Light

Prayer in the Evening
St. Augustine (354–430)

Watch, O Lord, with those who wake,
or watch, or weep this night,
and give Your angels charge
over those who sleep.

Tend to Your sick ones, O Lord Jesus Christ;
rest Your weary ones, bless Your dying ones,
soothe Your suffering ones, shield Your joyous ones,
and all for Your love's sake. Amen.

The Perfect Woman

Demands for Perfection

Who is the perfect woman? Are you? Everywhere we look, we discover that we are facing myriad demands for perfection, whether it be in the home, in the workplace, in the community, or even in the parish. Sometimes we inadvertently place demands upon ourselves. We want to measure up. It seems as if it's what we should do. After all, it appears that the "perfect" woman has it all—the perfect husband, the perfect family, perfect looks, the perfect home, and the perfect everything else. The advertising world entices us to buy a certain face cream for a wrinkle-free complexion and a particular makeup for just the right glow. Countless weight-loss diets, pills, exercise machines, and gimmicks clamor for our attention. For what? To be a size "zero"? The way I look at it, a size zero equals nothing. Therefore, there is no such thing as a size zero! So, why do women chase after impossible standards for supposed perfection?

The simple fact that we are women subjects us to countless expectations—from society, from our families, and from our peers. And these societal pressures begin early in life. Our culture subjects young, impressionable girls to crazy demands that can be overwhelming. It's impossible for girls to miss the idealized female body image because it's plastered all over the mass media.

Our tween-age and teenage girls are brainwashed by Hollywood, runway, television, Internet, and glossy magazines into believing that being a certain clothes size will solve all their problems and guarantee bliss in their lives. They are not necessarily aware of the industry trick of airbrushing that distorts the presentation of physical beauty and of what might be realistically attainable. We can help! Parents and grandparents and all those who mentor children should do their best to let them know what true beauty is. We can impress upon them that they must not worry about what others say so that they can be confident in their own skin. Clear, consistent boundaries provide a safety net and help our youth to make wise choices. Continual open communication and encouragement can reassure these precious girls that they can come to us anytime. Our love for them and our example of stability and faith in God will speak volumes.

We could write a whole book on the "perfect woman" starting with our Blessed Mother and going over all the demands for perfection that we women face and how to sort through them all to achieve a true inner peace. I have touched upon a few of the demands and problems and will provide suggestions.

Allow me to set the record straight: it might seem ironic that women who struggle for perfection can discover that they feel less and less adequate. They never measure up. They might have bought into the world's lopsided notions about a woman's worth, and they struggle to come to terms with what society expects of them. Sadly, they are not listening to their hearts and to what God wants. Often these women who are running after some kind of perfection become utterly exhausted in trying to prove their worth to the world. They haven't found peace in striving for the perfect physique, in working out at the gym, in the decor of their homes, in their kids' grades, or even in their relationship with the Lord. Is it ever perfect enough? Running after perfection might land us in the therapist's office, looking for peace and wondering why we aren't happy—or perfect!

Our good Lord is not asking us to measure up to some crazy, unobtainable standard of perfection, a youthful, wrinkle-free appearance, or a perfect manicure. He wants our hearts and our love in wholehearted surrender. He will work out the rest if we just trust Him.

Prayer of Surrender

St. Augustine (354–430)

Lord Jesus, let me know myself and know You,
and desire nothing save only You.

Let me hate myself and love You.
Let me do everything for the sake of You.
Let me humble myself and exalt You.
Let me think of nothing except You.

Let me die to myself and live in You.
Let me accept whatever happens as from You.
Let me banish self and follow You,
and ever desire to follow You.

Let me fly from myself and take refuge in You,
that I may deserve to be defended by You.
Let me fear for myself; let me fear You,
and let me be among those who are chosen by You.

Let me distrust myself and put my trust in You.
Let me be willing to obey for the sake of You.
Let me cling to nothing save only to You, and let me
be poor because of You.
Look upon me, that I may love You.
Call me that I may see You, and forever enjoy You.
Amen.

By Dawn's Early Light

A Tangled Web

Army wife Karen Smith, who will remain anonymous, has been involved in military life for more than twenty-nine years. She met her husband when he was in college on an ROTC scholarship. "We were married in October 1989 and set off for his first assignment in Oklahoma," she said. Karen is involved with the Military Council of Catholic Women (MCCW) and is active in her parish ministry as well as in the Catholic Women of the Chapel (CWOC), the school PTO, military unit activities, and Alcoholics Anonymous (AA). Spending time with her family, participating in Bible studies, being outdoors in God's creation, hiking near her home in the woods of Germany, and doing spiritual reading inspire Karen's heart.

Karen talked to me about some of the pressures and demands of military life when she and her family lived at West Point. Born to parents in their forties and growing up as the youngest of six, with older siblings in college, Karen explained, "I always felt I was in the wrong family and wrong body. I was the caboose." All of Karen's friends had young parents. "My mother spent most of my childhood in a deep depression with periodic hospitalizations." Karen's father was "a stoic man who worked hard and had impossibly high standards." To him, depression was considered a weakness of character. Throughout her childhood years, Karen felt "unnoticed" amid the dysfunction around her. She eventually found a need to cultivate "modes of transportation," she said, to escape the pain she felt. She ate compulsively and felt "fat and unhappy." Her brothers had "endless ammunition to terrorize me," she said. Karen later sought attention when out of the house and in school. "I think all of this laid the groundwork for my adult mode of transportation—alcohol," she recalled. "It was the perfect escape from any negative feelings: loneliness, depression, loss, sadness, fear," she explained. These are some of the issues that women associated with the military experience—"in spades!" she exclaimed.

Living in a Fish Bowl

Karen fell in love with a man whom God would use to help her "truly understand and experience the depths of God's grace and love," she told me. But first, there was a battle to be fought, which we will get into in more depth a bit later. For now, Karen said, "True to type, I married a man who adores me and who grew up in an alcoholic family." She went on to explain the demands of military life, living in sort of a "fish bowl," and how they always had to "present a happy, shiny, strong exterior," even when they experienced major life traumas and many relocations.

In the civilian world, a young family will most likely live in a neighborhood with a variety of people of many backgrounds, ages, and occupations. Some might never get to know their neighbors well, while some may be more outgoing and sociable. Karen said, "All can draw strength from the wisdom and encouragement of elder neighbors." People who live in such a community "can also be anonymous if they choose," and "their homes are a refuge from work, school, and social issues." For the most part, this is commonplace for civilians.

But for Karen and countless other military women and families, it's not so. They are in "constant competition," she said. "In the military world, we often live in communities based on rank." Explaining her experience at West Point, she said, "We lived in a square of thirty-two townhouses, all occupied by male active-duty captains with wives and children. I felt like a senior in high school!"

Next came the demands for perfection and the race to be the best. "We all had the same floor plan, same yard, same rank." Because of this, Karen explained, "We were in a never-ending race to have the nicest car in the driveway, the nicest yard, the most spectacular decor, the smartest kids, the most athletic kids, the best-looking spouse, and the most upwardly-mobile husband."

She emphasized the stress and pressure of the intense standards: "*No one* showed weakness in any form." This kind of living arrangement is difficult, but, according to Karen, it's made worse by its occurring in the small world of the military. It's extremely challenging in terms of privacy and the need to keep up appearances.

Then the unthinkable happened. Karen's husband was passed over for Major, and "word spread like wildfire!" At one point, she had a neighbor who became suicidal when he was passed over for a higher rank.

We need to pray for military families whose lives seem to be in a pressure cooker.

A Vibrant Life of Faith and Balance

Severe panic set in suddenly one day for Army wife Kim Miller. It was during her husband's third deployment. Kim had known her husband, Geoff, a Major in the Army, since high school. Geoff was always interested in serving his country and attended college on an ROTC scholarship. His family had a long history of service. Kim said, "I feel like I was on this path with him the whole time." Geoff has been on active duty in the Army for fifteen years thus far. Kim serves on the Worldwide Board for the MCCW, is involved in moms' groups at her parish, volunteers at her children's school.

She recalled, "I experienced a severe panic attack. It was toward the end of what had been a long, stressful, nine months, and everything I had been tamping down just sort of bubbled up." It came totally out of the blue, but she said, "Luckily, I was with friends and family and had some great care getting through it." Though it was frightening not to have the control she felt she needed, Kim was forced to rely on God and her friends and family to help her. She said, "It was scary to feel like I wasn't able to take care of everything I was supposed to be taking care of." Calling to mind that experience and other tough times in the military, including some relocations, Kim said, "My family back home, my military family, and my faith are the rocks that get me through." She certainly counts her many blessings. "My family and my husband's family are amazingly supportive and loving and always there for us when we need them. My faith keeps me grounded and also gives me a way to link into a new community anytime we move."

While countless women must contend with a persistent barrage of issues and demands, they also strive to find a healthy balance in their lives. No doubt, military women have their own unique demands to juggle and grapple with. Many Christian military women join faith-sharing groups and surround themselves with like-minded women to bolster their religious convictions and to discuss pressing issues. It's extremely helpful to stay connected to the wider faith community as well as the wider military community.

Kim recalled, "I was a pretty lazy Catholic when my husband, who is not Catholic, and I got married." But something interesting happened after Kim decided to move a bit out of her comfort zone to try something new. After their first daughter was born, her family moved to a new duty station. Kim said, "I reached out to our local Catholic Women of the Chapel group (CWOC)." Kim's faith grew in leaps and bounds as she spent time with the other faith-filled women. She said, "The growth I have experienced since I walked through the door to my first CWOC gathering has been huge." Kim is thankful that the blessings have benefited her entire family. "The growth hasn't just been mine," she added. "Our whole family has become much more involved with and committed to living our Faith." Kim is also a part of an Army Spouses Group, which she says, "keeps us connected to our Army roots!"

Exercise for Sanity and Health!

In addition to connecting with like-minded people and sharing the Faith, physical exercise is a healthy outlet for some stresses. Among other benefits, regular exercise can make you feel happier, lead to weight loss, help your bones and muscles, can increase your energy level, help you sleep better, reduce your risk for chronic disease, help your skin, and even help your brain health and memory. Now, that is a long list of benefits! I think we will all admit, though, that exercise requires effort on our part. As they say, "No pain, no gain!"

Exercise can be a lifesaver. "There is no pill that comes close to what exercise can do," says Claude Bouchard, director of the human genomics laboratory at Pennington Biomedical Research Center in Louisiana. "And if there was one, it would be extremely expensive."[3] It's always best to check out new exercise

---

[3] Mandy Oaklander and Heather Jones, "7 Surprising Benefits of Exercise," *Time*, September 1, 2016, http://time.com/4474874/exercise-fitness-workouts/.

programs with your doctor and to start easy and work your way up to more intensity.

Kim Miller enjoys running for exercise, to clear her head. She ran cross-country in high school and in college. She told me, "While I am not very fast these days, I find running the best, most therapeutic way to clear my mind and work through anything I am struggling with. It's sort of like a physical form of prayer." She explained, "I don't run with headphones, so I just sort of give it all over to God and let Him work things out for me while I run."

All kinds of military stresses can pop up on any given day. To keep her sanity, Kim explained, "Running is a huge outlet for me. I probably don't do it enough, but when I make time to run, I always feel restored."

True Beauty and a Mother's Vocation

Army wife Diane Joyce Bridon has been involved with the military for more than nineteen years. She told me about a struggle she went through with regard to her weight and her poor self-image. She said, "I used to think that because I was overweight, I was inadequate in everything that I would do. My spouse never made me feel that way; just the culture of this world did." The bombardment of unrealistic demands for women is overwhelming.

Diane shared with me that it was when she was feeling "inadequate" that she read one of my books for Catholic mothers. She said, "After reading *Grace Cafe*[4] I realized that I needed to em-

---

[4] Donna-Marie Cooper O'Boyle, *Grace Cafe: Serving Up Recipes for Faithful Mothering* (North Haven, CT: Circle Press, 2008). The second edition has been retitled *Catholic Wisdom for a Mother's Heart*.

brace motherhood in a different light — a joyful state. I learned ways to pray when I was doing mundane chores. I realized that motherhood and being a 'domestic operations manager,' as Dan calls me, is my vocation, and it is a very important vocation."

Many mothers fail to realize the God-given gift that motherhood truly is. Untold mothers have been crushed by our culture, which often measures a woman's worth by the size of her paycheck and not by the fact that within her vocation of love, she is raising precious little saints to Heaven!

Diane took immediate steps to help improve her attitude and overcome her struggles. "I began playing uplifting religious songs when I cooked and did the dishes." It worked! She said, "I began to feel joyful in my day. I felt happy inside. I began to feel God's Holy Spirit present with me in my daily walk." She was grateful and was not the only one who was noticing a difference and happy for it. "My children began to notice and pointed out the change in me, as well as my spouse." Even more, "I could feel the true beauty of God's divine love living in me, and with that I felt *beautiful!*" This was truly a breakthrough for Diane. "I learned what true beauty really is, being a mother and emulating our Blessed Virgin's vocation."

Prayer to Deal Well
with Demands for Perfection

Dear Lord, Jesus,
You know my life.

You know me through and through —
every hair on my head is counted.
I cannot hide from You.
You know my every thought and struggle.

Please help me to sort through
all the distractions and false promises
of the world, so that I won't fall
into the countless snares of the evil one.

Please keep me safe
and help me to protect my family
from the evil influences of the world
and to guide them steadily to You. Amen.

Communion Prayer

St. Peter Julian Eymard (1811–1868)

Oh, yes, Lord Jesus, come and reign!
Let my body be Your temple,
my heart Your throne,
my will Your devoted servant;
let me be Yours forever,
living only in You and for You! Amen.

The Eucharist

The Eucharist is the source and summit of our lives as Catholics. St. Teresa of Calcutta said that she and the Missionaries of Charity absolutely needed to receive the broken Body of Jesus in the Eucharist every morning at Holy Mass in order to have all they needed to go out and serve the broken bodies of the poor. She also made sure that she and the sisters all made a daily Holy Hour of adoring Jesus in the Blessed Sacrament to nourish their hearts and souls.

Even if you are not a religious sister, God still calls you to a life of holiness. Receiving Jesus in the Eucharist and adoring Him in the Blessed Sacrament is a sure way to attain that goal. I believe that being with Jesus in adoration brings a deep peace to the soul. If you cannot make a Holy Hour, try your best at least to stop by a church or chapel to spend even ten or fifteen minutes with the Lord as often as possible. Don't hesitate to bring your family, too. Our Lord awaits your visits and no doubt has many graces for you.

Spiritual Communion

Attributed to St. Francis of Assisi (1181–1226)

*Anytime you cannot receive Jesus in the Eucharist,
a Spiritual Communion is beneficial.*

I believe that You, O Jesus,
are in the Most Holy Sacrament.
I love You and desire You.
Come into my heart.

The Perfect Woman

I embrace You.
O, never leave me.

May the burning and most sweet
power of Your love,
O Lord Jesus Christ, I beseech You,
absorb my mind that I may die
through love of Your love,
who were graciously pleased
to die through love of my love. Amen.

Before the Blessed Sacrament

The Angel of Peace at Fatima (Fall 1916)

Most Holy Trinity,
Father, Son, and Holy Spirit,
I adore Thee profoundly.

I offer Thee the Most Precious Body, Blood,
Soul, and Divinity of Jesus Christ,
present in all the tabernacles of the world,
in reparation for the outrages, sacrileges,
and indifferences whereby He is offended.

And through the infinite merits
of His Most Sacred Heart
and the Immaculate Heart of Mary,
I beg of Thee the conversion of poor sinners. Amen.

By Dawn's Early Light

Anima Christi (Soul of Christ)

*This prayer, which originated in the fourteenth
century, is generally prayed after receiving Holy
Communion but can be prayed anytime.*

Soul of Christ, sanctify me.
Body of Christ, save me.
Blood of Christ, inebriate me.
Water from Christ's side, wash me.
Passion of Christ, strengthen me.
O good Jesus, hear me.

Within Thy wounds hide me.
Suffer me not to be separated from Thee.
From the malicious enemy defend me.

In the hour of my death call me
and bid me come unto Thee
that I may praise thee with Thy saints
and with Thy angels,
forever and ever. Amen.

I Love You, O My God

St. John Vianney (1786–1859)

I love You, O my God,
and my only desire is to love You
until the last breath of my life.

I love You, O my infinitely lovable God,
and I would rather die loving You,
than live without loving You.

I love You, Lord,
and the only grace I ask
is to love You eternally.

My God, if my tongue cannot say
in every moment that I love You,
I want my heart to repeat it to You
as often as I draw breath. Amen.

Act When Visiting the Most Holy Sacrament
St. Alphonsus Liguori (1696–1787)

My Lord Jesus Christ, who for the love which You bear
us, remain night and day in this sacrament full of compassion and love, awaiting, calling, and welcoming all
who come to visit You, I believe that You are present in
the Sacrament of the Altar.

I adore You from the abyss of my nothingness, and I
thank You for all the graces that You have bestowed
upon me and in particular for having given me Yourself
in this sacrament, for having given me Your most holy
Mother Mary as my advocate, and for having called me
to visit You in this church.

By Dawn's Early Light

I now salute Your most loving Heart; and this for three ends: first, in thanksgiving for this great gift; second, to make amends to You for all the outrages that You receive in this sacrament from all Your enemies; and third, I intend by this visit to adore You in all the places on earth in which You are present in this sacrament and in which You are the least reserved and the most abandoned.

My Jesus, I love You with all my heart. I grieve for having hitherto so many times offended Your infinite goodness. I purpose by Your grace never more to offend You.

And now, miserable and unworthy though I be, I consecrate myself to You without reserve; I give You and renounce my entire will, my affections, my desires, and all that I possess.

Henceforward, dispose of me and of all that I have as You please. All that I ask of You and desire is Your holy love, final perseverance and the perfect accomplishment of Your will.

I recommend to You the souls in Purgatory, and especially those who had the greatest devotion to the most Blessed Sacrament and to the most Blessed Virgin Mary. I also recommend to You all poor sinners.

Finally, my dear Savior, I unite all my affections with the affections of Your most loving heart, and I offer them, thus united, to Your eternal Father, and beseech Him in Your name to vouchsafe for Your love, to accept and grant them. Amen.

Radiating Christ

Blessed John Henry Cardinal Newman (1801–1890)

After the example of their foundress, St. Teresa of Calcutta, the Missionaries of Charity pray this prayer every day after receiving Holy Communion at Mass.

Dear Jesus, help me to spread Your fragrance wherever I go.

Flood my soul with Your spirit and life. Penetrate and possess my whole being so utterly, that my life may only be a radiance of Yours.

Shine through me, and be so in me that every soul I come in contact with may feel Your presence in my soul. Let them look up and see no longer me, but only Jesus! Stay with me, and then I shall begin to shine as You shine, so as to be a light to others.

The light, O Jesus, will be all from You; none of it will be mine. It will be You, shining on others through me. Let me thus praise You the way You love best, by shining on those around me.

Let me preach You without preaching, not by words but by my example, by the catching force of the sympathetic influence of what I do, the evident fullness of the love my heart bears to You. Amen.

By Dawn's Early Light

On Being Still

Can I be still—
even for a little while each day—
and drink up God's graces while
meditating on His great love for me?

Prayer for Five Graces

St. Alphonsus Liguori (1696–1787)

Eternal Father, Your Son has promised that You would
grant all the graces we ask of You in His name. Trusting in this promise, and in the name and through the
merits of Jesus Christ, I ask of You five graces:

First, I ask pardon for all offenses I have committed, for
which I am sorry with all my heart, because I have offended Your infinite goodness.

Second, I ask for Your divine Light, which will enable
me to see the vanity of all the things of this earth, and
see also Your infinite greatness and goodness.

Third, I ask for a share in Your love, so that I can
detach myself from all creatures, especially from myself,
and love only Your holy will.

Fourth, grant me the grace to have confidence in the
merits of Jesus Christ and in the intercession of Mary.

Fifth, I ask for the grace of perseverance, knowing that
whenever I call on You for assistance, You will answer my

call and come to my aid; I fear only that I will neglect to turn to You in time of need, and thus bring myself to ruin.

Grant me the grace to pray always, O Eternal Father, in the name of Jesus. Amen.

God Is My Strength and My Salvation

At the beginning of this chapter I quoted Archbishop Sheen: "Maybe I can find Christ on the battlefield, too." Take some time to ponder areas of your life that are in need of transformation. In dealing with difficult issues, can you discover "Christ on the battlefield" of your military service or on the home front? Conversion of heart is not a once-in-a-lifetime occurrence. It should be a daily experience as we go deeper into our prayer conversations with our Lord.

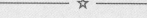

Lord, Enlighten My Heart!

Dear Lord, Jesus,
please enlighten my heart and soul
with Your graces and blessings!
Help me to be the woman I should be—
an example of holiness—
and to possess a generous heart
to glorify and praise You. Amen.

2

Patron Saints of the Military

All men desire peace,
but very few desire those things
that make for peace.

—Thomas à Kempis (1380–1471),
The Imitation of Christ 3, 25

The saints have much to teach us! You'll find some patron saints for the military in this chapter. Learn more about them and beg their intercession for yourself and your family. The *Catechism of the Catholic Church* tells about the amazing "cloud of witnesses" we have in the saints (Heb. 12:1):

> The witnesses who have preceded us into the kingdom (cf. Heb. 12:1), especially those whom the Church recognizes as saints, share in the living tradition of prayer by the example of their lives, the transmission of their writings, and their prayer today. They contemplate God, praise him, and constantly care for those whom they have left on earth. When they entered into the joy of their Master, they were "put in charge of many things" (cf. Matt. 25:21). Their intercession is their most exalted service to God's plan. We can and should ask them to intercede for us and for the whole world. (2683)

In *Veritatis Splendor*, St. John Paul II wrote about seeking the wisdom of the saints for strength and joy on our journey:

> In particular, the life of holiness which is resplendent in so many members of the People of God, humble and often unseen, constitutes the simplest and most attractive way to perceive at once the beauty of truth, the liberating

force of God's love, and the value of unconditional fidelity to all the demands of the Lord's law, even in the most difficult situations. For this reason, the Church, as a wise teacher of morality, has always invited believers to seek and to find in the saints, and above all in the Virgin Mother of God "full of grace" and "all-holy," the model, the strength, and the joy needed to live a life in accordance with God's commandments and the Beatitudes of the Gospel.[5]

In *The Lives of the Fathers, Martyrs, and Other Principal Saints*, by the Reverend Alban Butler, we read some very stirring words about soldiers who were martyrs, about the fact that sanctity is attainable in every walk of life, and about the treasures of virtues and martyrdom they can achieve. In defense of soldiers, Butler wrote:

Although many dishonor the profession of arms by a licentiousness of manners, yet, to show us that perfect sanctity is attainable in all states, we find the names of more soldiers recorded in the martyrologies than in almost any other profession. Every true disciple of Christ must be a martyr in the disposition of his heart, as he must be ready to lose all, and to suffer anything, rather than to offend God. Every good Christian is also a martyr, by the patience and courage with which he bears all trials. There is no virtue more necessary, nor of which the exercise ought to be more frequent, than patience. In this

---

[5] St. John Paul II, *Veritatis Splendor* (*The Splendor of Truth*) (August 6, 1993), no. 107.

mortal life we have continually something to suffer from disappointments in affairs, from the severity of the seasons, from the injustice, caprice, peevishness, jealousy, or antipathy of others; and from ourselves, in pains either of mind or body. Even our own weaknesses and faults are to us subjects of patience. And as we have continually many burdens, both of our own and others, to bear, it is only in patience that we are to possess our souls. This affords us comfort in all our sufferings and maintains our souls in unshaken tranquility and peace. This is true greatness of mind and the virtue of heroic souls. But, alas! Every accident ruffles and disturbs us; and we are insupportable even to ourselves. What comfort should we find, what peace should we enjoy, what treasures of virtue should we heap up, what an harvest of merits should we reap, if we had learned the true spirit of Christian patience! This is the martyrdom and the crown of every faithful disciple of Christ.[6]

---

[6] Alban Butler and Charles Butler, *The Lives of the Fathers, Martyrs, and Other Principal Saints*, 12 vols. (London: C. Dolman, 1854), vol. 4.

By Dawn's Early Light

Prayer to My Patron Saint

O heavenly Patron,
whose name I have the honor to bear,
pray earnestly at all times to God for me,
confirm me in the faith,
strengthen me in virtue,
defend me in the battle of life,
so that conquering the enemy of my soul,
I may deserve to be rewarded
with everlasting glory. Amen.[7]

[7] Jacquelyn Lindsey, *Catholic Family Prayer Book* (Huntington, IN.: Our Sunday Visitor, 2001), 43.

Our Lady of Loreto, Patroness of Aviators and Astronauts

The title Our Lady of Loreto for Mary, the Mother of God, refers to the holy house where she was born and where the angel Gabriel visited her at the Annunciation. Tradition holds that angels transported that house from the Holy Land to Loreto, Italy, in the thirteenth century, and for this reason, Our Lady of Loreto is patron of aviators and astronauts. Over the centuries, countless pilgrims—including many popes—have visited the Holy House of Loreto, and thousands of miracles have been attributed to Mary and recorded there.

Prayer to Our Lady of Loreto

Our Lady of Loreto, our glorious mother, we confidently turn to you. Receive our humble prayer. Humanity is troubled by great evils, which it seeks to overcome on its own, and is in need of peace, justice, truth, and love, yet thinks it can find these divine realities away from your Son.

O mother! You, who carried the Divine Savior in your immaculate womb and lived with Him in the Holy House that we venerate on the Loreto Hill, grant us the grace to seek Him and imitate His example, who leads us to salvation. Amen.

By Dawn's Early Light

St. Barbara, Martyr, Patroness of Artillery and Engineers

St. Barbara (third century) was an early Christian Greek martyr who was born in Heliopolis, Phoenicia. Because of some doubt about the history of St. Barbara, she was removed from the General Roman Calendar, but not from the Catholic Church's list of saints.

St. Barbara's father, Dioscorus, was a pagan. After Barbara's mother's death, her father kept her shielded from the world by locking her in a high tower. Only her pagan teachers were allowed to see her. Eventually, Barbara gained freedom from the tower, learned about Christianity, and was secretly baptized. Dioscorus was furious about her baptism and grabbed his sword to strike her. Barbara fled and was later found by her father, who had her tortured, but she would not renounce her Christian Faith. Her father handed her over to Martianus, the prefect of the city, and the two of them continuously beat Barbara. Miracles occurred in which Barbara's wounds from the abuse were continuously cured.

On December 4, 306, she was martyred, when Dioscorus himself beheaded her. Lightning struck and killed both Dioscorus and Martianus, and it is believed that it was a divine punishment for the murder of St. Barbara. Her tomb in Valentinus became a site of miracles. St. Barbara is the patroness of artillerymen, armorers, military engineers, gunsmiths, tunnelers, miners, and those working with cannons and explosives. She is venerated by Catholics whose work puts them in danger and is invoked against thunder, lightning, and accidents arising from explosions of gunpowder. The U.S. Army Field Artillery Association and the U.S. Army Air Defense Artillery Association maintain the Order of St. Barbara as an honorary society within the military.

Patron Saints of the Military

Prayer to St. Barbara

St. Barbara, you were raised
to the altar of sainthood
and you behold
the face of God in heaven.

Please intercede before
the Most Holy Trinity for me
(*mention your request*)
and pray that I can be steadfast
in my faith as you have always been. Amen.

St. Elizabeth Ann Seton, Patroness of the United States Sea Services

Elizabeth Ann Bayley Seton (1774–1821) is the first native-born American to be canonized by the Catholic Church. She lived in an upper-class family in New York. In 1794, she married William Seton and experienced a comfortable life for a time, but she would later be besieged with many losses and deaths in her family.

When William's father died, the young couple assumed responsibility for the seven half-brothers and sisters and the family's import business. Eventually, William's health and business failed. He and Elizabeth sailed to Italy, hoping that the mild climate would restore William to health. Despite all efforts, William died of tuberculosis while there. Elizabeth's consolation was that William had recently turned to God. She stayed in Italy for a time and was drawn to the Catholic Church, which she joined in 1805.

Upon returning to America, Elizabeth eventually founded a religious order and continued to raise her children. She developed a great love for teaching and serving others. On March 25, 1809, Elizabeth pronounced her own vows of poverty, chastity, and obedience, binding for one year. From that time, she was called Mother Seton. She became stricken with tuberculosis but continued to guide her children. The Rule of the sisterhood she founded was based on the Rule that St. Vincent de Paul had written for his Daughters of Charity in France. It was formally ratified in 1812. Within six years, the sisters had established two orphanages and a second school. Today, six orders of religious sisters can trace their origins to Mother Seton's initial foundation.

In 1821, at the age of forty-six, Mother Seton died. She was beatified by Pope John XXIII on March 17, 1963, and canonized by Pope Paul VI on September 14, 1975. Her feast day is January 4.

St. Elizabeth Ann Seton Prayer

Lord God, You blessed Elizabeth Seton
with gifts of grace as wife and mother,
educator and foundress,
so that she might spend her life
in service to Your people.
Through her example and prayers
may we learn to express our love
for You in love for our fellow men and women.
We ask this through our Lord Jesus Christ,
Your Son, who lives and reigns
with You and the Holy Spirit,
one God, forever and ever. Amen.

St. Erasmus (Elmo), Patron of Sailors

St. Erasmus (died ca. 303), affectionately known as St. Elmo, is the patron of those who suffer from abdominal pain and those who make their living at sea. Sailors' devotion to him came about because, during storms at sea, they noticed blue electrical discharges dancing like lightning in their rigging and masts. They accepted this as a sign of St. Erasmus's protection. This has been referred to as "St. Elmo's fire."

In the late second century, St. Erasmus was a bishop of Formia (located between Rome and Naples). He is the patron saint of Gaeta, where he moved after Formia burned. He is considered one of the Fourteen Holy Helpers—a group of saints whose intercession was sought around the time of the bubonic plague. St. Erasmus was martyred under the emperor Diocletian.

Prayer to St. Erasmus

Lord God, You gave the Church St. Erasmus,
raising him to the altar of sanctity.
May he intercede for us in all our needs,
especially in keeping our soldiers protected at sea.
May Your Church enjoy unending peace
and be secure in Your protection,
through our Lord Jesus Christ,
Your Son, who lives and reigns with You
in the unity of the Holy Spirit,
one God, forever and ever. Amen.

St. George, Patron of Soldiers and Cavalry

There are many legends about St. George, who lived in the third or fourth century. He is the patron of England, Portugal, Germany, Aragon, Genoa, and Venice. He was most likely martyred about 303 in the Palestinian city of Lydda. St. George was said to have been seen helping the Franks at the Battle of Antioch in 1098. He became more popular in Europe after the success of this battle in Europe, leading military men to implore his intercession. It is said that St. George appeared in an apparition to King Richard I in his expedition against the Saracens. This was a tremendous encouragement to the soldiers, and shortly after they defeated the enemy. St. George's feast day is April 23.

----------- ☆ -----------

Prayer to St. George, Martyr

Dear St. George,
God has raised you to sainthood.
Please guide me with your inspiration
to be courageous in all the battles I face.
Please petition the Holy Trinity
to hear my prayer:
(*mention your request*). Amen.

By Dawn's Early Light

St. Ignatius of Loyola, Patron of Soldiers

St. Ignatius of Loyola (1491–1556) was born into a noble family in Northern Spain. He is a patron of soldiers and the founder of the Society of Jesus.

Íñigo López de Loyola grew up to be a handsome, heroic, yet headstrong knight consumed with extravagance and the desire for his own glory during political upheavals in Spain in the 1500s. He was driven to near suicide after a cannon ball shattered his leg and he was forced to be still while recuperating from the multiple surgeries the injury required. During his convalescence, Íñigo reluctantly began to read books on Jesus and the saints, for those were the only books available in the castle. Despite his initial aversion to these books, he became interested in them and grew intrigued by the heroic lives of the saints and by the ways in which they courageously lived out their Faith. He vowed to live the remainder of his life as a soldier for Jesus and Mary.

Íñigo planned to go to Jerusalem to fight to take back the Holy City from its Turkish Muslim invaders. On the way, however, he realized that the saints who had impressed him had used no weapons except for their deep faith. He then visited a Benedictine monastery and left his sword at an altar dedicated to Mary.

In time, Íñigo experienced a total transformation and conversion of heart, turning completely away from his dark past to embrace a radically austere life as a beggar and a quiet, disciplined contemplative—going on to instruct many others spiritually, and eventually to become one of the greatest saints of all time—St. Ignatius of Loyola!

Known for his *Spiritual Exercises* and his founding of the Jesuit Order, St. Ignatius underscores the grave importance of turning away from sin, nourishing our souls with truth, and staying close to Jesus, Mary, and the saints, who lead us to Heaven. His feast day is July 31.

Prayer of Self-Offering
St. Ignatius of Loyola (1491–1556)

Take, O Lord, and receive my entire liberty,
my memory, my understanding, and my whole will.
All that I am and all that I possess
You have given me:
I surrender it all to You to be
disposed of according to Your will.
Give me only Your love and Your grace;
with these I will be rich enough,
and will desire nothing more. Amen.

Prayer Against Depression
St. Ignatius of Loyola

O Christ Jesus,
when all is darkness
and we feel our weakness and helplessness,
give us the sense of Your presence,
Your love, and Your strength.
Help us to have perfect trust
in Your protecting love

and strengthening power,
so that nothing may frighten or worry us,
for, living close to You, we shall see your hand,
Your purpose, Your will in all things. Amen.

Prayer from St. Ignatius of Loyola's
Spiritual Exercises

Eternal Lord of all things,
I feel Your gaze on me.
I sense that Your Mother stands near,
watching, and that with You are
all the great beings of Heaven:
angels and powers and martyrs and saints.

Lord Jesus, I think You have put a desire in me.
If You will help me, please,
I would like to make my offering.
I want it to be my desire and my choice,
provided that You want it, too,
to live my life as You lived yours.

I know that You lived
as an insignificant person
in a little, despised town.
I know that you rarely tasted luxury
and never privilege,
and that You resolutely refused
to accept power.

I know that You suffered rejection by leaders,
abandonment by friends, and failure.
I know.
I can hardly bear the thought of it all.

But it seems a toweringly wonderful thing
that You might call me to follow You
and stand with You.
I will labor to bring God's reign
if You will give me the gift to do it. Amen.

By Dawn's Early Light

St. Joan of Arc, Patroness of Soldiers and Military Leaders

Joan of Arc (1412–1431), a subject of many books, movies, and plays, was born in France to well-to-do peasant parents. Joan loved the sacraments and had a heart for the poor. In 1424, at twelve years old, this simple peasant girl began having visions of St. Margaret, St. Catherine, and St. Michael. She heard St. Michael tell her that she needed to go to King Charles VII to support him and help him rid France of the English.

Despite her young age, during the many battles of the Hundred Years' War, Joan was instrumental in recapturing Orleans, Rheims, Paris, and numerous other towns from the English. The angry English declared her a heretic.

Joan was captured near Compiègne and was sold to the English. She was placed on trial for heresy and witchcraft, was interrogated, and was condemned to death for her crimes against the English and as a heretic, sorceress, and adulteress. Joan refused to retract her statements that it was the saints who appeared to her and spoke to her. In 1431 in Rouen, nineteen-year-old Joan was burned at the stake. She asked for a cross to be made that she put on her dress while she was burned. A priest held up another cross for Joan to gaze upon during her martyrdom. Witnesses attest to her composure and courage.

Joan's ashes were dispersed in the Seine River. It is said that her heart did not burn and was thrown into the river with her ashes so that there wouldn't be any relics. In 1456, Pope Callixtus III declared that Joan was innocent of her crimes and was now considered a martyr. Joan was beatified in 1909 and canonized in 1920. To St. Joan of Arc is ascribed the prayer "I fear nothing, for God is with me." Her feast day is May 30.

Novena Prayer to St. Joan of Arc

Opening Prayer

Eternal Father, You gave us St. Joan of Arc
through Your infinite love and mercy for us.
We humbly ask that You send down Your Holy Spirit
upon us, as your Spirit is the intermediary
by which the Word goes forth from Your lips
and reaches the ears of the faithful.
Allow me to be a witness to Your Son
Jesus Christ, just as St. Joan of Arc was.

O Jesus, grant me the courage to do Your will,
that I may be in one accord with our Father in Heaven.
I thank You for the gift of Your love,
which I hope to understand fully one day.

Petition Prayer
Pray nineteen Our Fathers,
followed by the following prayer:

St. Joan of Arc,
by your powerful intercession,
hear and answer me.

St. Joan of Arc,
I ask you now to fight this battle
with me by prayer,
just as you led your troops to victory in battle.
You, who were filled with
the Holy Spirit and chosen by God,
help me this day with the favor I ask:
(*mention your request*).

By Dawn's Early Light

Grant me by your
divine and powerful intercession
the courage and strength I need
to endure this constant fight.
O St. Joan, help me to be victorious
in the tasks God presents to me.

I thank you and ask you
for your continuing protection
of God's people.

Closing Prayer

Sweet St. Joan,
plead for me before the throne
of Almighty God, that I may be deemed
worthy to be granted the request I have asked.
Help me, St. Joan, to be more like you
in the attempt to love our Lord
with all my heart, soul, and mind.
Through your guidance and prayer
help me to be a truly devout
and loving Christian, that I may
both know and see the will of God.

Help me now St. Joan, in my time of need.
I ask that you may always be near me
guiding me closer each day to Jesus.
Thank you, St. Joan,
for having heard my prayer. Amen.

St. John of Capistrano, Patron of Military Chaplains

St. John (1385–1456) was born in Capistrano, Italy, the son of a former French or German knight. His father died young, and his mother raised and educated John. He learned Latin and studied civil law and Church law in Perugia. He became a prominent public figure and was appointed governor of the city at the young age of twenty-six.

In addition to being involved in a political career, St. John of Capistrano carried out extensive missionary journeys and made efforts to reunite separated Eastern Christians with Rome. After a war broke out between Perugia and Malatesta, he was captured and imprisoned. He prayed intensely during his captivity and had a vision of St. Francis of Assisi. who told him to join the Franciscans. After his release from prison, St. John petitioned for a release from his marriage in order to enter religious life. He entered the Franciscan community at Perugia in 1416 and was ordained a priest in 1420. He and St. James of the March were fellow students under St. Bernardine of Siena, who inspired St. John to institute the devotion to the Holy Name of Jesus and His Mother Mary.

After his ordination, St. John traveled and preached tirelessly throughout Italy, Germany, Bohemia, Austria, Hungary, Poland, and Russia, drawing huge crowds, one exceeding 126,000 people! After one of his sermons, more than 100 university students entered the Franciscan Order. His presence was requested far and wide, and many miracles of conversion are attributed to his preaching and prayers. He would always say, "Not to us, O Lord, not to us, but to Thy name give glory." St. John also established numerous communities of Franciscan renewal.

When Mohammed II threatened Vienna and Rome, Pope Callixtus III commissioned seventy-year-old St. John to preach and lead a crusade against the invading Turks. In 1456, leading seventy thousand Christians, St. John gained victory in the great battle of Belgrade against the Turks. He died at Ilok, Hungary, three months later. Many miracles occurred after his death. He was canonized in 1690.

Now invoked as a patron of military chaplains, St. John of Capistrano was praised by St. John Paul II in a 2002 General Audience for his "glorious evangelical witness" as a priest who "gave himself with great generosity for the salvation of souls." His feast day is October 23.

Prayer to St. John of Capistrano

Lord,
you raised up St. John of Capistrano
to give Your people comfort in their trials.
May Your Church enjoy unending peace
and be secure in Your protection,
through our Lord Jesus Christ, Your Son,
who lives and reigns with You
in the unity of the Holy Spirit,
one God, forever and ever. Amen.

St. Martin of Tours, Patron of Soldiers, Infantry, and Cavalry

St. Martin (316–397) is one of the most beloved saints in the history of Europe. He was born to pagan parents in Sabaria, Upper Pannonia (a province comprising northern Yugoslavia and Western Hungary). His father was an officer in the Roman Army and was transferred to North Italy—a providential move because it enabled young Martin to learn about Christianity. He was enthralled with learning the Faith and even at a young age considered becoming a hermit in the desert. But, because his father was in the military, Martin was required to enter the Army at the age of fifteen. He was stationed in Amiens, in Gaul, and lived more like a monk than a soldier. He was a generous young man and cared much for the poor, giving a generous portion of his paycheck to the unfortunate.

It was in Gaul that a most amazing miracle occurred, for which St. Martin is perhaps the most famous and which dramatically changed his life. The young Martin came upon a sparsely dressed poor man shivering from the freezing temperature. At once, Martin took off his own woolen cloak, slashed it in two with his sword, and wrapped the man in half of it. He put the other half around himself. That night, Jesus appeared to Martin in a dream. He was wearing the half garment that Martin had given the poor man. Jesus said, "Martin, a catechumen, has clothed me with this garment." Moved by this, Martin knew without doubt that he had to join the Church immediately. He remained in the military for another two years and then sought a discharge from the Roman Army because he felt called to do more with his life.

Martin was accused of cowardice for asking to leave the military, but he replied that he would face the enemy without weapons—that he was not afraid and would simply seek protection from the sign of the Cross. It turned out that the Germans sought peace, so Martin's pleas were unnecessary. He received his discharge. Martin's faith increased, and he lived a life of severe asceticism. His prayer life was intense. He built what might have been the first monastery in Gaul. He lived for many years as a monk and, through his prayers, raised two people from the dead. He became the third bishop of Tours but continued to live a simple life, going about preaching and driving out pagan practices.

Always concerned about helping souls and getting to Heaven, St. Martin of Tours told his followers, shortly before he died in November of 397, "Allow me, my brethren, to look rather toward Heaven than toward the earth, that my soul may be directed to take its flight to the Lord, to whom it is going."[8] His feast day is November 11.

Prayer to St. Martin of Tours for Soldiers

Dear well-beloved saint,
you were first a soldier like your father.
Converted to the Church,
you became a soldier of Christ,
a priest, and then a bishop of Tours.
Lover of the poor, and model for pagans
and Christians alike, protect our soldiers at all times.
Make them strong, just, and charitable,
always aiming at establishing peace on earth. Amen.

---

[8] "St. Martin of Tours," Catholic News Agency, http://www.catholicnewsagency.com/saint.php?n=50.

Prayer of St. Martin of Tours

Based on St. Martin's prayer to God before his death

Lord, if Your people still have
need of my services,
I will not avoid the toil.
Your will be done.
I have fought the good fight long enough.
Yet if you bid me continue to hold
the battle line in defense of Your camp,
I will never beg to be excused from failing strength.
I will do the work You entrust to me.
While You command,
I will fight beneath Your banner. Amen.

Prayer for the Intercession of St. Martin of Tours

Blessed St. Martin of Tours,
full of the Spirit of the Lord
always having inexhaustible charity for the needy;
full of love and generosity,
when you saw the beggar who was freezing from cold,
without knowing that in truth he was Christ,
did not hesitate to give him half of your cape,
and did not give it completely to him
since the other half belonged to the Roman Army:
you, who did not seek recognition
but only to favor your neighbor,
found glory before the Lord.

By Dawn's Early Light

And when the Savior appeared to you
dressed with the half cape
so as to express appreciation for your gesture
and told you, "Today you covered me with your mantle,"
you decided no longer to serve the Army
but to dedicate your life to God
and to the salvation of souls,
being from then on a propagator of the Faith
and a holy man totally dedicated
to whoever was in need.

Glorious St. Martin,
you who worked miracles and prodigies,
who with joy, amiability, and
the most exquisite goodness
won over the hearts of all
and never ceased to work for their well-being:
give me your hand and help me to be freed from
all lack and scarcity that today
afflicts me and weighs me down.

Glorious St. Martin, my blessed patron,
I humbly ask you with great faith
that you attain from God,
the fount of all mercies
that my ways on this earth,
my work and my toils,
may be cleansed
and begun with purity of purpose.

In the name of the omnipotent God,
St. Martin of Tours,

remove all that harms me
and give me work and prosperity.
O blessed relief, give me your saintly protection;
assist me, I beg you, in these difficult times:
(*with much faith, ask for what you need*).

You, noble St. Martin,
who have miraculous power
take my supplications with haste to the heavens;
ask for my home all that is good;
may sorrows, ruins, and miseries leave,
and may the Lord deign that I merit
good fortune in my work (business)
and, with it, abundance and prosperity,
so I may give freely to all in need.

St. Martin, blessed Bishop of Tours,
may your virtues and charity
accompany me always.
I will not cease to pray to you
and to thank Almighty God
for all the favors granted;
and I promise to be charitable
and giving with all my brothers and sisters in need.

St. Martin please intercede for me;
free and protect all my loved ones and me
from all that is evil.

Amen.

*Pray the Creed, the Our Father,
the Hail Mary, and the Glory Be.*

St. Maximilian Kolbe, Patron of Prisoners

St. Maximilian Kolbe (1894–1941) was a Polish Conventual Franciscan Friar who was sent to the Auschwitz death camp for hiding Jews during World War II. In retaliation for an escape from the camp, ten prisoners were chosen by the Nazi guards to be starved to death. Kolbe heroically volunteered to die in place of a stranger who was a family man. He was canonized as a martyr on October 10, 1982, by Pope John Paul II.

Raymund Kolbe was born into a relatively poor family in Zdunska Wola, in the Kingdom of Poland (then part of the Russian Empire). Raymund's father was German and his mother Polish. In 1914, his father was captured by the Russians and hanged for fighting for an independent Poland.

When he was twelve years old, Raymund had a vision of the Blessed Mother. He recounts, "That night I had asked the Mother of God what was to become of me. Then she came to me holding two crowns, one white, the other red. She asked me if I was willing to accept either of these crowns. The white one meant that I should persevere in purity, and the red that I should become a martyr. I said that I would accept them both." The following year, he and his brother Francis joined the Conventual Franciscans.

Raymund was given the religious name Maximilian and was admitted as an initiate in 1910. In 1914, he took his final vows as a monk. After a brief period in Krakow, Poland, he studied in Rome, earning doctorates in philosophy and theology. He was ordained a priest at age twenty-four and, in 1919, returned to the newly independent Poland, settling in the monastery of Niepokalanów near Warsaw.

Kolbe was deeply devoted to the Blessed Virgin Mary. He founded the Militia of the Immaculata, to fight evil with the witness of a good life, prayer, work, and suffering, and published the religious magazine *Knight of the Immaculata* to preach the Good News to all nations. He also established a "City of the Immaculata" to house seven hundred of his Franciscan brothers and later founded another house in Nagasaki, Japan. Both the Militia and the magazine would end up reaching more than a million members and subscribers. Kolbe also opened a temporary hospital to aid those in need and he continued to provide shelter in his monastery for refugees.

During his last days, Kolbe encouraged the other prisoners who were sentenced with him to death by starvation, leading them in prayers to Our Lady and exhibiting a peaceful demeanor. His feast day is August 14.

Novena Prayer to St. Maximilian Kolbe

O Lord Jesus Christ, who said,
"Greater love hath no man than this,
that he lay down his life for his friends,"
through the intercession of St. Maximilian Kolbe,
whose life illustrated such love, we beseech You
to grant us our petitions:
(*mention your requests*).

Through the Militia Immaculata movement,
which Maximilian founded,
he spread a fervent devotion to Our Lady
throughout the world.
He gave up his life for a total stranger
and loved his persecutors,

giving us an example of
unselfish love for all men —
a love that was inspired by
true devotion to Mary.

Grant, O Lord Jesus, that we too
may give ourselves entirely without reserve
to the love and service of our heavenly Queen
in order better to love and serve
our fellowman in imitation of
Your humble servant Maximilian. Amen.

Pray three Hail Marys and a Glory Be.

Novena Prayer for
St. Maximilian Kolbe's Intercession

Merciful God, You made St. Maximilian Kolbe one of
the foremost Catholic evangelists of the difficult twentieth century. Through the Militia of the Immaculata
movement that he founded, he implanted the truths of
the Immaculate Conception and Your merciful plan for
us in countless hearts, thus moving them to full conversion in faith and hope, to perfect obedience and union
with the Heart of Jesus, and to complete observance of
the New Covenant.

You made him fruitful through carrying the cross of
suffering with dignity and hope, loving his persecutors,
and giving up his life for a total stranger. Through his

intercession, grant us our petitions (*mention your requests*). Give us a like dignity and hope in our sufferings and sacrifices, and if it will glorify You, heal us of all our infirmities, both physical and spiritual.

Finally, enable us to follow St. Maximilian's example of effective Catholic evangelism with Mary for the return to You of all the masses of mankind, and of every individual person, family, society, and culture of our time and of all times to come. Amen.

Prisoner's Prayer to St. Maximilian Kolbe

O prisoner-saint of Auschwitz, help me in my plight.
Introduce me to Mary, the Immaculata, mother of God.
She prayed for Jesus in a Jerusalem jail.
She prayed for you in a Nazi prison camp.
Ask her to comfort me in my confinement.
May she teach me always to be good.
If I am lonely, may she say, "God is here."
If I feel hate, may she say, "God is love."
If I am tempted, may she say, "God is pure."
If I sin, may she say, "God is mercy."
If I am in darkness, may she say, "God is light."
If I am unjustly condemned, may she say, "God is truth."
If I have pain in soul or body, may she say, "God is peace."
If I lose hope, may she say:
"God is with you all days,
and so am I." Amen.

By Dawn's Early Light

St. Michael the Archangel, Patron of Marines, Paratroopers, and Police

St. Michael the Archangel—whose name means "Who is like God?"—is often invoked by military Christians and perhaps also by those who do not pray frequently, specifically because this archangel is known for his great strength and protection. It was St. Michael who led the army of angels to cast Satan and his evil rebellious angels into Hell (Rev. 12:7). St. Michael will use a sword of justice to separate the good from the evil at the end of time.

St. Michael has come to the rescue in various circumstances throughout history and has even been said to have helped on battlefields. One such time was in 590 when, because of a great plague that had stricken Rome, Pope St. Gregory the Great led a procession through the streets of Rome as an act of penance, seeking forgiveness and praying to atone for sin. St. Michael suddenly appeared at the tomb of Hadrian (which is now Castle Sant' Angelo, near St. Peter's Basilica) and sheathed his sword, which indicated the end of the plague. St. Gregory later built a chapel at the top of the tomb, and to this day a large statue of St. Michael stands there.

During most of the twentieth century, the faithful recited the prayer to St. Michael at the end of every Mass. This devotion was begun by Pope Leo XIII (d. 1903), who, one day in 1884, suddenly fell to the floor after celebrating Mass. A doctor was called immediately, but he could not find the pope's pulse. The Holy Father was feared dead. Pope Leo suddenly awoke, however, and exclaimed, "What a horrible picture I was permitted to see!" He had received a vision that vividly showed the coming century comprising much sorrow and war.

In his vision, God gave Satan the choice of one particular century in which to do his worst work against the Church. The devil chose the twentieth century. The Holy Father was so shaken from the vision that he immediately put pen to paper to compose the prayer to St. Michael the Archangel, a much longer version than the one most Catholics know by heart. In 1886, Pope Leo ordered this prayer said at the conclusion of Mass. Later, when Pope Paul VI issued the Novus Ordo of the Mass in 1968, the St. Michael prayer was suppressed.

One hundred years after Pope Leo composed this famous prayer, in the spring of 1994, St. John Paul II urged the faithful once again to offer the prayer to St. Michael the Archangel after Mass and at other times. It was not a mandate, but rather an encouragement. In his *Regina Caeli* message of Sunday, April 24, 1994, the Holy Father said, "May this prayer strengthen us for the spiritual battle mentioned in the Letter to the Ephesians: 'Be strong in the Lord and in his mighty power' (Eph. 6:10)." The pontiff called to mind the image of St. Michael and Pope Leo XIII's writing of the powerful prayer. He reminded the faithful that "although this prayer is no longer recited at the end of Mass, I ask everyone not to forget it and to recite it to obtain help in the battle against the forces of darkness and against the spirit of this world."

Let us call on this great archangel each day for protection and guidance, asking him to shield us from the evil tactics of the devil, who never sleeps and who strives to drag all souls to Hell.

By Dawn's Early Light

Prayer to St. Michael

St. Michael the Archangel,
defend us in battle.
Be our defense against the wickedness
and snares of the devil.
May God rebuke him,
we humbly pray,
and do thou,
O Prince of the heavenly hosts,
by the power of God
thrust into Hell Satan
and all evil spirits
who prowl about the world
seeking the ruin of souls. Amen.

Another Prayer to St. Michael

O glorious prince St. Michael,
chief and commander of the heavenly hosts,
guardian of souls, vanquisher of rebel spirits,
servant in the house of the Divine King
and our admirable conductor,
you who shine with excellence
and superhuman virtue, deliver us from all evil,
who turn to you with confidence
and enable us, by your gracious protection, to
serve God more and more faithfully every day. Amen.

Act of Consecration to St. Michael the Archangel

O most noble Prince of the Angelic Hierarchies, valorous warrior of Almighty God and zealous lover of His glory, terror of the rebellious angels, and love and delight of all the just angels, my beloved archangel St. Michael, desiring to be numbered among your devoted servants, I today offer and consecrate myself to you and place myself, my family, and all I possess under your most powerful protection.

I entreat you not to look at how little I, as your servant, have to offer, being only a wretched sinner, but to gaze rather with favorable eye at the heartfelt affection with which this offering is made, and remember that if from this day onward I am under your patronage, you must during all my life assist me and procure for me the pardon of my many grievous offenses and sins, the grace to love with all my heart my God, my dear Savior Jesus, and my sweet Mother Mary, and to obtain for me all the help necessary to arrive to my crown of glory.

Defend me always from my spiritual enemies, particularly in the last moments of my life.

Come then, O glorious Prince, and succor me in my last struggle, and with your powerful weapon cast far from me into the infernal abysses that prevaricator and proud angel that one day you prostrated in the celestial battle. Amen.

St. Sebastian, Martyr, Patron of Soldiers

An early Christian martyr, St. Sebastian (d. ca. 288) was born in Narbonne, Gaul, in Southern France to Italian parents. He was raised and educated in Milan, Italy. Though Sebastian was opposed to fighting, he joined the Roman Army to be of service to other Christians who were being persecuted by the Romans. He often visited them in prison. Sebastian was promoted to serve in the Praetorian Guard to protect Emperor Diocletian.

While serving in this capacity, he came across Marcus and Marcellian, twin Christian brothers who had been imprisoned because of their refusal to worship Roman gods. Sebastian encouraged them in their refusal, as well as their parents, who wanted their sons to renounce their Christianity. Sebastian converted many prominent people and reportedly healed a soldier's mute wife by making the Sign of the Cross on her. Many other instances of healing are attributed to him.

Emperor Diocletian discovered Sebastian's efforts to help Christians and ordered him to be put to death. Sebastian was tied to a stake and used as target practice. Filled with arrows, he was left for dead but was nursed back to health after being found alive by a Christian woman. Sebastian eventually regained his health but would not flee to safety. Instead he went in search of Diocletian to confound him with the fact that he was still alive. When Sebastian encountered the emperor, he rebuked him for persecuting Christians. The amazed Diocletian regained his composure and then ordered this dead man walking to be beaten to death and to be thrown into the sewers.

A Christian woman named Lucina discovered the martyr's body and had Sebastian secretly buried in catacombs beneath Rome. Later, his remains were moved to a basilica in Rome. St. Sebastian, the patron of soldiers, athletes, and those who desire a saintly death, is commonly invoked as a protector against the plague, possibly because he defended Rome against the plague in 680.

Prayer in Remembrance of St. Sebastian
Gregorian Sacramentary

O God, who did bestow on blessed Sebastian,
Your martyr, such wonderful strength
of valor in his sufferings for You:
grant us, after his example, to condemn,
for love of You, all earthly prosperity, and
to dread no sort of adversity. Amen.

Prayer to St. Sebastian for Athletes

Dear Commander of the Roman emperor's court,
you chose also to be a soldier of Christ
and dared to spread faith in the King of Kings,
for which you were condemned to die.

Your body, however, proved athletically strong
and the executing arrows extremely weak.

So, another means to kill you was chosen,
and you gave your life to the Lord.

May athletes always be as strong in their faith
as you, their patron saint, so clearly have been. Amen.

Servant of God Vincent R. Capodanno, M.M.

Servant of God Vincent R. Capodanno (1929–1967) was the recipient of many honors. During his second Vietnam tour of duty, on September 4, 1967, with the Third Battalion, Fifth Marines, he made the ultimate heroic sacrifice. After hours of heavy fighting from a North Vietnamese ambush, Father Capodanno, seriously injured and unarmed, spotted a wounded Marine corpsman pinned down by an enemy machine gunner and ran to his aid to administer medical and spiritual attention. The enemy opened fire, and Father Capodanno died from twenty-seven bullet wounds after faithfully performing his final act as a good, faithful servant of God.

Prayer to Obtain a Favor through the Intercession of Father Capodanno (1)

Archbishop Timothy P. Broglio

Almighty and merciful God,
look with love on those
who plead for Your help.
Through the intercession of Your servant
Father Vincent Capodanno, missionary
and Catholic Navy chaplain,
grant the favor I earnestly seek:
(*mention your request*).
May Vincent,
who died bringing consolation
to the Marines he was privileged

to serve on the field of battle,
intercede in my need as I pray
in the name of the Father, and of the Son,
and of the Holy Spirit. Amen.

Prayer to Obtain a Favor through the Intercession of Father Capodanno (2)
Cardinal Edwin F. O'Brien

May God, who has offered healing and strength
through the hands of His only Son, Our Lord,
and through Christ's many servants,
grant me the favor of His healing hand
through the intercession of His servant
Father Vincent Capodanno,
priest, missionary, and chaplain,
who always sought to heal and comfort
the wounded and the dying on the field of battle.
May I be granted this request on my own field of battle
I pray, in the name of the Father, and of the Son,
and of the Holy Spirit. Amen.

Cardinal Nguyen Van Thuan:
The Influence of a Saint

Cardinal Nguyen Van Thuan (1928–2002) was a Vietnamese bishop who was arrested by the Vietnamese government shortly after being appointed bishop. While he was in prison for thirteen years, he wrote about the Faith. He said, "Whereas a person attached to sin can bring division and contributes to that which harms the world, a person attached to a holy life can bring the Word of God and contributes to the life of humanity. The Lord lives and acts through saints and nothing stands in the way of the power of divine grace."

He noted that "many people are surprised by the weakness of their sight: they cannot see what the saints contemplated, or perceive what the saints so easily distinguished. This is because saints look at everything with God's eyes; they measure their existence in God's light; they do not give in to confusion, because they live in reality and in truth."

In thinking about the value of the present moment of life and not wasting time, this saintly man wrote on a scrap of paper while in prison:

> The saints lived on earth as much as I do.
> The saints were swept along
> by the same current of time.
> Their days were twenty-four hours long
> and not one minute more!
> Their lives were not longer in years:
> Francis Xavier died at the age of forty-six,
> Thérèse of the Child Jesus at twenty-four,
> and Rose of Lima at thirty-one.
> But the years they lived

were incomparably intense and concentrated,
because they recognized that time
has the value of eternity.
God works through the saints
who collaborate with God.
How much we must esteem a single moment
of the Lord's work!

We build holiness in the present moment
not by turning to the past or anticipating the future.
That is why the saints treasured the present moment;
without neglecting a single instant, they made
each moment a response of their whole being
to God's love.

The saints lived in the present as in an immense ocean
of peace because they already lived in that unending
present of eternity.[9]

---

[9] Phanxicô Xaviê Văn Thuận Nguyễn, *Prayers of Hope, Words of Courage* (Boston: Pauline Books and Media, 2002), 72.

St. Joseph

St. Joseph is a protector of the Universal Church. We should get to know him and ask for his intercession. St. Teresa of Avila said, "Go especially to Joseph, for he has great power with God." She also said that St. Joseph never failed her. In my own life, he has been very instrumental. I consider him to be one of my biggest heroes!

The litany of St. Joseph, the foster father of Jesus and the spouse of the Blessed Mother, is one of only six approved by the Church for public and private use. It speaks of the humble St. Joseph's attributes and beseeches his help and protection. When this litany is prayed in public, the congregation responds to a leader with the words in italics.

Litany of St. Joseph

Lord, have mercy.
Christ, have mercy.
Lord, have mercy.
Christ, hear us.
Christ, graciously hear us.

God the Father of Heaven, *have mercy on us.*
God the Son, redeemer of the world, *have mercy on us.*
God the Holy Spirit, *have mercy on us.*
Holy Trinity, one God, *have mercy on us.*

Holy Mary, *pray for us.*
St. Joseph, *pray for us.*
Renowned offspring of David, *pray for us.*

Patron Saints of the Military

Light of Patriarchs, *pray for us.*
Spouse of the mother of God, *pray for us.*
Chaste guardian of the Virgin, *pray for us.*
Foster father of the Son of God, *pray for us.*
Diligent protector of Christ, *pray for us.*
Head of the Holy Family, *pray for us.*
Joseph most just, *pray for us.*
Joseph most chaste, *pray for us.*
Joseph most prudent, *pray for us.*
Joseph most strong, *pray for us.*
Joseph most obedient, *pray for us.*
Joseph most faithful, *pray for us.*
Mirror of patience, *pray for us.*
Lover of poverty, *pray for us.*
Model of artisans, *pray for us.*
Glory of home life, *pray for us.*
Guardian of virgins, *pray for us.*
Pillar of families, *pray for us.*
Solace of the wretched, *pray for us.*
Hope of the sick, *pray for us.*
Patron of the dying, *pray for us.*
Terror of demons, *pray for us.*
Protector of Holy Church, *pray for us.*

Lamb of God, who takes away the sins of the world,
Spare us, O Lord.

Lamb of God, who takes away the sins of the world,
Graciously hear us, O Lord.

Lamb of God, who takes away the sins of the world,
Have mercy on us.

V. He made him the lord of his house.
R. *And ruler of all his substance.*

Let us pray.
O God, who in thine unspeakable providence
didst vouchsafe to choose blessed Joseph
to be the spouse of thine own most holy mother:
grant, we beseech thee, that we may deserve
to have him for our intercessor in heaven,
whom we reverence as our defender on earth:
who livest and reignest world without end. Amen.

God Is My Strength and My Salvation

St. John Paul II said "War should belong to the tragic past, to history: it should find no place in humanity's agenda for the future."[10] That is certainly what we hope and pray for. But right now, we live with the reality of a darkened world. Let us keep our eyes on Heaven and its rewards and do all that we can to be a brilliant light of faith to others who are struggling to find their way. The saints can help us. Let's call upon them often, seeking their powerful intercession.

[10] William Madges, *Vatican II: Forty Years Later*, College Theology Society Annual Volume (Maryknoll, NY: Orbis Books, 2006), 229.

3

Take Up Your Cross

*Jesus has now many lovers of the heavenly
kingdom but few bearers of his cross.*

—Thomas à Kempis (1380–1471),
The Imitation of Christ 2, 11

Suffering is oftentimes a great mystery. Why is it necessary? we might wonder. How do we endure it? Why should we? Thomas à Kempis wrote, "Without doubt it is better for you ... to be tried in adversities than to have all things as you wish."[11] Why can't we have all the things we wish? Most importantly, it is because God is the Divine Physician and He knows what is best for our souls. If we had everything we wanted, would we be as prayerful as we should? Would we be too busy for God? Those "things" we want might very well drag us down to Hell rather than help to get us to Heaven.

Thomas à Kempis also wrote, "The more spiritual progress a person makes, so much heavier will he frequently find his cross, because as his love increases, the pain of his exile also increases."[12] But he reassures us: "With God, nothing that is suffered for His sake, no matter how small, can pass without reward." Clearly, Catholics and Christians have a different way of looking at suffering from the rest of the world. Our Lord Jesus said, "If any want to become my followers, let them deny themselves and take up their cross and follow me. For those who want to save their life will lose it, and those who lose their life for my sake will find it. For what will it profit them if they gain the whole world but forfeit their life? Or what will they give in return for their life? (Matt.

[11] Thomas à Kempis, *The Imitation of Christ*, 3, 30.
[12] Ibid., 2, 12.

16:24–26). Are we greater than our Master, who carried His Cross and died for us? To be a Christian means to strive to be like Jesus and to desire to offer our lives in love and service to others.

Offer It Up!

Some might remember the old phrase "Offer it up!"—a means to tell kids and others to stop complaining about certain inconveniences or pains and to offer them to God instead. It's not merely a scapegoating tactic or something to distract a person from his suffering or to belittle his pain. Yes, suffering hurts and can take us by complete surprise. Often, we want to run and hide from it. If we don't understand the reason for suffering and pain, it most likely will be even harder to bear. Archbishop Fulton Sheen remarked, "If pain and suffering had no reason, then we can be sure our divine Lord would never have embraced them."[13] Though pain, loss, and suffering can be utterly devastating, when we discover and begin to understand the deeper meaning of their existence in our lives, surprisingly, we can even begin to embrace them, knowing that we can become co-redeemers with our Lord. Many of the saints have expressed the importance of offering up our pain and suffering to God and asking Him to transform it all for the good. However, we shouldn't gripe and complain all the while. Archbishop Sheen explained, "By patiently accepting each pain in union with his Cross, we become redeemers with a small 'r' as he is a Redeemer with a capital 'R.'"[14]

[13] *Fulton Sheen's Wartime Prayer Book* (Manchester, NH: Sophia Institute Press, 2003), 37.
[14] Ibid.

Jesus told us that we must take up our cross and follow Him. Further, there is much power and meaning in suffering when it is offered lovingly to God. "If we suffer, we shall also reign with him" (2 Tim. 2:12, KJV). Let us remember to ask our good Lord to grant us the graces necessary to accept His holy will in our lives and to carry our crosses with love. My dear friend Mother Teresa said we should "give whatever God takes from us and take whatever he gives us with a big smile."[15] Let's pray to do that. We can have peace of soul when we strive more wholeheartedly to serve our Lord.

Your Cross

St. Francis de Sales (1567–1622)

The everlasting God has
in His wisdom foreseen
from eternity the cross
that He now presents to you
as a gift from His inmost heart.

This cross He now sends you
He has considered with His all-knowing eyes,
understood with His divine mind,
tested with His wise justice,
warmed with loving arms,

---

[15] Mother Teresa, *Mother Teresa : Come Be My Light: The Private Writings of the "Saint of Calcutta,"* 1st ed. (New York: Doubleday, 2007).

By Dawn's Early Light

and weighed with His own hands
to see that it be not one inch too large
and not one ounce too heavy for you.

He has blessed it with His Holy Name,
anointed it with His consolation,
taken one last glance at you
and your courage,
and then sent it to you from Heaven,
a special greeting from God to you,
an alms of the all-merciful love of God.

Take Up Your Cross

Many Kinds of Battles

War is said to be ugly. And stress is a killer. War affects those who fight it, those back home who support their soldiers, and their loved ones who are constantly worrying about them. So many uncertainties are associated with military life. And military personnel of every rank and branch have seen the ugly terrors of war and continually come face-to-face with situations that most of us could never even imagine. We need to support our soldiers with much prayer—not only while they are fighting, but when they are back home trying to transition into a so-called normal life, whatever that may entail. Soldiers are affected by stress and strain—physically, emotionally, and mentally. They fight a war not only on the battlefield but also in their hearts and minds. We need to pray for their spiritual, emotional, and physical protection. Their families need many prayers as well.

My brother Gary, who served in Vietnam, hardly said a word about the war. In fact, when he came home, he sat in the same old chair in our family living room for hours on end, watching senseless television shows—most likely to get his mind off the horrors he had witnessed. He did say once that he would often encounter children in Nam selling candy bars to the American soldiers during the day, and at night time these children would be chained to machine guns firing away at them. Perhaps one of the greatest difficulties Gary experienced because of the Vietnam War was that he came home to discover that his fiancée had left him for another man while he was out there fighting in jungles to serve his country.

In my memoir, *The Kiss of Jesus*, I tell the stories of crazy experiences along my crooked path through life and how our dear Lord was with me even in all of my dark nights. I was held captive by a man with automatic weapons when I was only about eighteen years old. The man was my fiancé, who had been a Marine and served in Vietnam. He snapped because of post-traumatic stress disorder (PTSD) and I bore the brunt of his affliction.

During the writing of this book, I met a woman whom I will call Janice. She purchased my memoir at a Catholic conference and took a look at the dust jacket. She read that I was once held captive by a Vietnam veteran and became intrigued. When she asked me to sign the book, she shared what had happened to her. She said she hadn't shared it with anyone. While she was pregnant, her husband, a Vietnam veteran, beat her up seven times. He had also snapped from PTSD. Janice managed to escape after her baby was born. War is terrible and affects our soldiers and their families more than we might believe.

Coming Home from Deployments

"Returning from deployment is often harder than deployment itself, but I really didn't see this one coming!" That's what Army wife Karen Smith told me. Karen's husband, an Army Colonel, was deployed in Romania for six months and Afghanistan for twelve. He returned to a new family dynamic—something that Karen didn't realize was happening while he was away. "Our oldest son had assumed the role of alpha male in the house and didn't take kindly to his dad trying to reclaim the role," Karen explained. Her son, fifteen at the time, had begun "to occupy the vacuum" that his father's absence created. He took an interest in assisting his siblings and his mother, helping with homework, and defusing tantrums. He was good at it, too!

"I hadn't seen what happened until this 'reintegration' period." The two of them would have to work it out. Karen added,

"My husband learned he had to be respectful and appreciative of our son's efforts even though he was only seventeen!"

Karen's son had become the "man" of the family in his father's absence. He knew how to motivate his brother and how to divert and discipline his younger sister. When his dad returned to the nest, Karen's son frequently told his dad, "That's *not* how it's done!" There were many clashes, according to Karen, who found herself stuck in the middle. "It took several uncomfortable months before the equilibrium returned."

Servant of God Archbishop Sheen reminds us, "Because there is a God, this war is not hell. God permits it to happen only for a greater good presently unseen. The war is more like Purgatory than hell, for through its refining flames we were meant to have the dross of our materialism burned away."[16]

Survivor Guilt: She Had Never Heard of It

Our hearts rejoice when our soldiers come back home safely to us and in one piece. We heartily welcome home our wounded soldiers, too, relieved that they are alive. Thank God! Yet, our soldiers have seen the terrors of war—things no one should have to see, experience, or bear in any way, shape, or form. Our soldiers and their families are very much affected by those things. We might not realize that one of the deeply scarring wounds that our soldier might suffer is "survivor guilt," which affects and debilitates countless soldiers who are desperately trying to transition back into some kind of "normal life." These poor soldiers feel guilty for having survived—for being alive! How tragic! On top of that, because they experience this kind of torture,

[16] *Fulton Sheen's Wartime Prayer Book*, 11.

their families suffer, too. Yet, many times, these soldiers can't put their finger on what is happening to them. They often suffer alone in their pain.

Sometimes called "survivor syndrome," survivor guilt is an element of post-traumatic stress disorder, but, of course, someone can experience this guilt without the diagnosis. The duration and intensity of survivor guilt varies with each individual, but the person feels guilty because he survived something when others did not or because someone died saving him, or he feels that he could have done something more to save someone, and so forth.

Army wife "Laura" (who wishes to remain anonymous) never expected her husband to go MIA—at least not in their own home. She shared her disconcerting experience with me. She explained that after returning from a deployment, her husband, "Keith" (who will remain anonymous), began to act very peculiar and had become distant, which caused her to fear for his well-being, but also for the health of their marriage.

Laura knew something was definitely not right with Keith, even though on the surface everything checked out okay. She shared, "He was dutifully fulfilling all of the roles of a father, soldier, and husband." She added, "He was doing a great job at work, and our kids were flourishing." Yet something was dreadfully wrong. His problems seemed to make their appearance in the dark of the night. That's when he went MIA! Laura said, "I noticed that my husband would wake up after midnight and spend hours out of bed." She was perplexed. What could he be doing? This Army wife secretly donned a "detective hat" and quietly observed over a few months' time. She said that when he was missing from their bed in the night, she "also noticed that his cell phone was missing from his nightstand." Night after night, Keith seemed to take on a strange personality, leaving the bedroom in secret and wandering around the house.

Is Something Wrong?

"Each time I asked if something was wrong, I was met with the mask of, 'I'm fine.' And to the outside world, he was; but I knew better." All kinds of scenarios were conjured up and acted out in Laura's imagination as she wrestled with this strange ghost each night. "As my husband disappeared from bed at night with his cell phone in tow, I started to spin worst-case-scenario *Lifetime* dramas in my head." She even began to blame herself for her husband's bizarre behavior. "I figured that if everything was 'fine,' with him, then something must be wrong with me." Unfortunately, Laura began to doubt herself. "Perhaps I was too fat, too dumb, or uninteresting?" The list went on and on. She thought, "Maybe he was interested in someone else." But, no matter the actual cause, Laura shared, "I grew distrustful. I was checking receipts, cell phone records, and Internet records for some horrible cause of the insomnia and disinterest in me."

Laura suffered terribly and didn't know what else she could do besides spying on and observing every single thing her husband did. Finally, she had had enough of all of it. She decided to turn to a priest. "I went to Confession with a military chaplain and confessed my mistrust, that I had made my husband's behavior all about me, that I was spinning myself into horrible hypotheticals about what could be causing the problem, and that I was snooping on my husband. Yes, snooping!" She was embarrassed, but contrite.

To Laura's relief, in addition to the many graces received, she was given something very valuable in the sacrament of Confession. "My priest gave me some wise counsel and then the most

By Dawn's Early Light

important penance ever: 'Talk to your husband.'" Laura left the confessional with grace and equipped with the confidence and Catholic tools necessary to face this problem head-on. She was not going to dance around it any longer. "I went home that evening, did the normal bedtime routine of bathing the kids, washing dishes, and packing sandwiches for the next day's lunches. Then, once the lights went out, I went into 'lay in wait' mode." Laura was determined to get to the bottom of it, no matter what it took. One sleepless night was not going to kill her. She was absolutely determined to find out. "I waited for my husband to wake up and start roaming the house, but this time I followed him." Yes, Laura was determined, but she still did not really want to confront Keith. Yet she had no choice: "Because my penance was to talk with him, I was convinced that I had to face whatever resided on the other side of this conversation." God would give her the grace.

"I found my husband, illuminated by the blue microwave clock, flipping through his phone, standing in our kitchen." She said, "I took his hand, pulled him down onto the couch, put on my 'stern mommy voice,' and said, 'What is going on?'" Keith kept up his front. "I'm fine" was his answer. "Really?" Laura asked. He shot back, "Yes, I'm fine." Laura couldn't accept that veiled answer. She told me, "Knowing that it was my penance to have the hard conversation, no matter how it might turn out, I set my eyes on him, lowered the tone of my voice and repeated, 'What is going on?'" punctuating each word. She waited. "Somewhere I read that if you wait for seven seconds of silence, someone will speak, so I waited."

Can We "Accept" War Fatalities?
Eventually, Keith's jaw started to quiver, and he said, "Okay. This is going to sound so stupid." Laura leaned in slightly and braced

herself. "For a split second, I saw a crazy *Lifetime* scenario flash across my mind, and I braced for the worst." Keith then let it all out—blow by blow. He told her that during their Christmas travels, he had seen the name of a college friend on a marble plaque that listed the names of alumni who had died in Iraq. Laura said, "My husband explained that he anticipated losing soldiers in his unit in war, and that while difficult, he had accepted those deaths and had come to terms with them." She continued, "He knew the missions that had led to combat deaths, and he was there to process those deaths with his unit."

It is not as easy as that, however. Although a soldier might "anticipate" that there will be losses, how do you actually "process" combat deaths? War always takes a toll on soldiers' hearts as well as on their families' hearts. Some war injuries don't show up for decades, as is sometimes the case of survivor guilt and other forms of PTSD. Laura explained that the name that Keith observed on the plaque was a college friend "with whom we had studied, laughed, drunk beer, and eaten cheap delivery pizza," she recalled. "This was also someone who had outperformed my husband in both academics and military exercises," Laura added.

As Keith explained his feelings about seeing his friend's name carved on that plaque, Laura began to understand his sleepless nights. She said, "To see this person's name listed as killed in combat, when my husband had survived, was difficult for him to process." That friend had died more than ten years prior, but, Laura explained, "This was the first time that my husband was confronted with this marble-carved reality. My husband couldn't sleep because he was feeling a sense of guilt for having lived, while our friend, who was so talented, had not."

Keith had suffered with the survivor guilt ever since seeing his friend's name on that plaque. Laura said, "He just could not stop feeling guilty because 'This shouldn't have happened.'" Thankfully, Keith explained that he was not contemplating hurting himself and that he was not reliving his own combat experiences. Laura was very relieved. She said, "So there we had it. The truth. My husband felt embarrassed that his guilt was, as he called it, irrational." But, because it was now out in the open, they could both learn from the uncomfortable and perplexing experience. Laura told him that she "thought it was a perfectly rational response to over sixteen years of military service in time of war." Laura distinctly remembers emphasizing to Keith, "Sixteen years of war is irrational! What you are feeling is completely rational."

What Next?
What to do next? They agreed that Keith would speak to a military priest whom he trusted. He'd do so the next day. It would be "a priest who had been with my husband when his unit lost a soldier the previous year," Laura told me. "This would not be the first time that they had worked through tragedy together." Laura followed up with her confessor, conveying all the details of her conversation with Keith. She had never heard of "survivor guilt" before her confessor reassured her that it must be what her husband had been suffering. Her confessor encouraged her to ask Keith to talk this out with a trusted individual, a counselor, priest, or confessor. Laura said, "For the past few months, my husband has been checking in with his priest, and he has started sleeping again." Laura is relieved that the mystery has been solved and that in time and with God's grace, her husband will heal and so will she. She added, "While he wakes up sometimes, I know why, and we are able to talk about how he is feeling and thinking."

This couple decided to revisit the plaque together. Sadly, they noticed that the name of another classmate and friend had been added in the previous few months. Loss of life is a very sad reality of war. But if you are a survivor, take heart and stay close to God. Don't blame yourself. Make it a point to speak to your family about how you are feeling. They love you and don't want you to suffer survivor guilt. If it is not appropriate to talk to a family member, then seek the confidence of someone you trust, and talk it through with that person.

The Sacraments Bring Hope, Healing, and Peace
There is help and great hope. In the case of Laura and Keith, the graces in the sacrament of Reconciliation came into play. The sacraments are so important to our journeys. We need to seek spiritual health and healing frequently through the sacraments of our Church and not hesitate to seek counseling also whenever warranted. Laura emphasized, "My marriage suffered because my husband and I were trying to face the effects of war independently and alone, seeking to be self-reliant. Once we relied on each other and the sacrament of Reconciliation, my husband's injury and our marriage was healed."

Laura reflected further on the experience that she and her husband shared over his survivor guilt. She concluded, "This experience has taught me that the injuries of war can be subtle and can manifest themselves at any time." She knew she needed help to be able to discern what was troubling her husband and what made her react to his strange behavior. She said, "I went to confession because I was contrite for mistrusting my husband, but I left charged with a duty to work on my marriage." Much good came out of the experience because Laura decided to seek help from the Church. Laura believes it was a grace to discover that she should work on her marriage. "My husband and I received the grace of reconciling our lack of communication and casting aside a false idea that he was supposed to be able to bear alone the troubles of a career served in a time of war without relying on his wife, or professionals." Laura added, "This is an aspect of our life that we will continue to process, but I'm grateful to our military priests who have helped us work through it and for the sacrament of Reconciliation, which brought us back to our marriage."

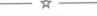

Prayer of St. Andrew

St. Andrew (first century) was martyred by being nailed to a cross. He loved Jesus so much that, as he was led to the place of his martyrdom, he cried out this prayer.

O good Cross,
made beautiful
by the body of the Lord:
long have I desired you,
ardently have I loved you,
unceasingly have I sought you out;
and now you are ready
for my eager soul.
Receive me from among men
and restore me to my Master,
so that He who,
by means of you,
in dying redeemed me,
may receive me. Amen.

Prayer of a Soldier

Joyce Kilmer (1886–1918)
Kilmer was an American writer, poet,
and convert to Catholicism who was killed
in combat in France during World War I.

My shoulders ache beneath my pack
(Lie easier, Cross, upon his back).

I march with feet that burn and smart
(Tread, Holy Feet, upon my heart).

Men shout at me who may not speak
(They scourged thy back and smote thy cheek).

I may not lift a hand to clear
My eyes of salty drops that sear.
(Then shall my fickle soul forget
thy Agony of Bloody Sweat?)

My rifle hand is stiff and numb
(From thy pierced palm red rivers come).

Lord, thou didst suffer more for me
Than all the hosts of land and sea.

So let me render back again
This millionth of thy gift. Amen.

By Dawn's Early Light

Battling Depression

As an Army wife, Lynda MacFarland has been involved in the military for thirty-six years and considers it a "vocation." She shared with me, "I had no idea when we began this journey that I would feel so strongly connected to the men and women who are in uniform and also to their families." When asked why she got involved in the military in the first place, Lynda exclaimed, "I married a soldier!"

Military life sometimes takes on a life of its own when one sets foot into it. It is at times a huge leap of faith with amazing graces and challenges lying right around the corner. Military life has certainly challenged Lynda, who said that "just getting through a year or longer deployments without bitterness toward God, your soldier, the Army, the nation who sends him into harm's way" is "a major triumph." She added, "Still praising, thanking, loving God and your soldier, and your country—those are triumphs!" Lynda attributes a "positive attitude of gratitude" as an aid to stay grounded, as well as "faith, family, and friends," or as she describes them, "the 3 Fs!"

Lynda said her faith is bolstered by her "faith studies, Catholic podcasts, and my own daughter and son, who remain faithful to the Catholic Church as adults." As well, "our awesome Military Council of Catholic Women conferences, faith community chapel groups, some great chaplains, and Gold Star families whose faith in God sustains them after the tragic loss of their loved one."

Through her military journey, Lynda grew to become a voice for the military. She said, "I am a strong, vocal, proactive advocate for our Army families, and it is a privilege to be so. I am grateful for the opportunity God has provided me." She told me that she believes that "we need to be honest with one another about our struggles, ask for prayers, and let others pray over us." Though military women have their own unique challenges, Lynda said, "Military women of faith are really just like all women of faith. We need to pray—talk to God—to keep that relationship vital and strong. God never wanders from us, but we sometimes wander from Him." She punctuated her point with an inspiring nudge: "Work together to enhance the quality of life of others."

As I mentioned, military life involves various battles—not simply the one being fought on the battlefield. Between two of her husband's deployments, Lynda struggled deeply with depression. She said, "I felt little to no comfort through the heavy, ugly oppression that engulfed me. I *knew* God loved me, but I couldn't *do* anything about it."

Lynda felt paralyzed. She felt a lack of interest in things. It was "not just a lack of enthusiasm, but a general malaise that most things that used to matter simply no longer did." Lynda also felt a lack of energy, plus a good deal of anxiety to go with it. Because of all of this, she didn't want to go anywhere or see anyone. "Truth be told," she said, "I didn't want to talk with anyone, either. And I certainly did not want to be 'cheered up.' In fact, that's not possible for someone who is clinically depressed," she said. "You can't just 'give yourself a good talking to' nor can anyone else help you to 'snap out of it'!"

After what she has been through, Lynda highly recommends speaking with a trained behavioral health professional. She found great help in doing so and added that, in addition, "prescribed antidepressant medication" can help make a difference.

Don't Drown in Lemonade—There Is help!

Lynda believes that "telling your loved ones about your struggle is crucial." It is hard sometimes to admit that we need help. "For me, it was extremely humbling to admit I needed help." Lynda is immensely grateful that she "bit the bullet" and did so, however. Admitting that something was wrong and reaching out to others for help completely rerouted Lynda's journey. She shared, "I have grown so much spiritually and emotionally because of that experience that I am grateful to have gone through that 'valley of death' so that I could become the person I am now."

Being a wife and mother, Lynda was accustomed to helping everyone else, but she had to help herself as well as allow others to help her. Now she is a great help to others who are struggling with depression and anxiety and says she "is the first one to suggest speaking to someone who can help as soon as possible." Throughout the painful ordeal, Lynda said she "never stopped talking to God in prayer and never believed He had abandoned me." Even with this knowledge, Lynda could not feel joyful. She came to recognize that she was missing something great. She was not complete.

"I was not living the life God intended me to live as His daughter and that was also making me depressed." She paused and said, "I did know that this wasn't how I should be. I was not the full expression of myself; I was not glorifying God with my life." Lynda recalled, "I am grateful that He gave me people in my life who brought me back to Him." Where did that begin? "It started with my own dear husband, and so that is why it's so important to tell your loved ones!" she exclaimed. Lynda wholeheartedly believes that one's family and true friends "are going to be the ones who help lead you back to the path of life and love and gratitude! They will be Jesus' hands and feet and voice for you!"

One time Lynda was talking with a group of military women just after hearing that their soldiers' year in Iraq would be extended. Everyone was understandably upset—in fact, pretty much devastated. Lynda told them, "There's an old saying that when life hands you lemons, you should make lemonade." She quickly added, "I don't know about you, but right about now, I'm *drowning* in lemonade."[17] Her fellow sisters wholeheartedly agreed, and some of them applauded Lynda.

Lynda later decided to write a book, *Drowning in Lemonade: Reflections of an Army Wife*, to help others to understand some of the negative effects of military life, such as anxiety, depression, and other mental problems that can affect spouses of deployed military personnel, but also equally significant, to stress the importance of our abiding faith in God and the hidden power in suffering when it is offered lovingly to God.

In the introduction to Lynda's book, Major Charles De Rivera of the Army stated, "More often than not, the spouse and/or parent in the rear is so concerned and emotionally enmeshed in caring for the deployed loved one that they do not practice health and wellness preventative measures of self-care." There is great help available. He added, "A behavioral health professional can help with the preventative coping skills before a situation becomes serious, and that is a good way to be proactive in dealing with one's emotional and psychological health."[18] Very wise words indeed.

In *Drowning in Lemonade*, Lynda explains:

The "lemons" are negative experiences; and if we accept them and praise God in spite of them and continue to

---

[17] Lynda MacFarland, *Drowning in Lemonade: Reflections of an Army Wife* (Austin, TX: Mary's Touch), 59–69.

[18] Ibid., xxi.

thank him for everything, we have just prepared the lemonade. To thank God for everything at all times, regardless of the situation, is to abandon yourself to his Will and trust that his only concern is for you.

Then the negative connotation of "drowning" (in lemonade) becomes an incredibly inviting desire to immerse yourself in the ocean of God's mercy, allowing him to do what's needed for your benefit.

Lynda says, "Reflect on Jesus' suffering. Unite your sufferings to his cross. It will benefit others, too. Because the sweet outcome, the resurrection and defeat of death, is worth it all to him. Try to thank God for your trials."[19]

Christ Has No Body

St. Teresa of Avila (1515–1582)

Christ has no body but yours,
No hands, no feet on earth but yours.

Yours are the eyes
with which He looks with
compassion on this world;

Yours are the feet
with which He walks
to do good;

[19] Ibid., 61–62.

Take Up Your Cross

Yours are the hands,
with which He blesses
all the world.

Yours are the hands,
yours are the feet,
yours are the eyes;
you are His body.

Christ has no body now but yours,
No hands, no feet on earth but yours.
Yours are the eyes with which He looks
with compassion on this world.

Christ has no body now on earth but yours.

By Dawn's Early Light

Stress and Strain on Marriage and Families

Military life is filled with all kinds of unique experiences. Some are amazingly joyful with regard to the patriotism and camaraderie of the soldiers and their families. Some are devastating and can rip marriages and families apart. Brenda Nonnweiler has been an Air Force wife for more than twenty-six years. Initially, she had applied to join the Navy but withdrew her application after meeting her future husband. Together they desired the chance of a college education and security for their future family. The military seemed like a good option for them. After Brenda's husband's first enlistment ended, having two children at that time, they wanted a steady pay check, "so we decided to stay in," she explained.

Brenda likes being involved with other military wives who share the same faith: "They know what I'm going through, or at least have a darn good idea, since their husbands and children are going through similar things that my husband and children are going through, and I can discuss things about my faith." And she is happy that she doesn't need to "defend why I want to pray a Rosary or go to the Blessed Sacrament Chapel." That "really helps," she explained. Brenda is involved in the MCCW and says, "I was hooked after I attended my first retreat in Ettal, Germany, in 2005. After that, I wanted to get involved to be close to these faith-filled women to fulfill a sense of 'giving back.'" Later, after being stationed in Oahu, Hawaii, Brenda helped to revitalize the local Catholic Women of the Chapel (CWOC) with weekly Bible studies and monthly activities.

To nourish her heart and soul, Brenda tries to spend "quality time with God." She enjoys her daily devotionals, prays the Liturgy of the Hours when she can, and tries to get to a couple of extra Masses per week. "My alone time with God gives me guidance, direction, and helps me identify and work on the many areas of growth that God is walking me through," she explained.

Brenda shared with me that her life "underwent a 180-degree direction change after attending the Rite of Christian Initiation for Adults (RCIA), and now my greatest help is the relationship I have with Jesus." She discussed some of the ups and downs of military life with me. Beginning on a positive note, she said, "Being involved in chapel activities helping others—women's ministry, especially, but also helping behind the scenes" has bolstered her faith. She added to that, "Learning more about the Catholic Faith and the history of the Church, attending Mass, receiving the Holy Eucharist, witnessing the actions and lives of holy people" impacts her life in a powerful way.

As an Air Force wife, Brenda experienced many relocations: once they lived in Germany for six years. Joel had ten assignments in a twenty-six-year span. Brenda further explained some of the difficulties. She said, "Along with uprooting our family every few years, the relatively low income afforded to airmen and junior NCOs caused many sleepless nights, wondering how we were going to make ends meet." It certainly takes a toll. She added, "Our lowest income occurred when our family was the youngest and needed the most health care."

"I Want a Divorce"

Brenda also experienced challenges that no wife should have to endure. Yet, by God's grace and the family's perseverance, they pulled through. She said she felt most vulnerable and devastated "when Joel asked for a divorce right after my mother died and in the middle of a PCS move." The family was scheduled to move to another state, and Brenda's siblings and father were paying their last respects to their mother. Brenda was also trying hard to help her father deal with his grief. She had a lot going on.

She shared, "One day my husband called and told me to 'stay in California, don't bother coming to Ohio' because he wanted a divorce." Joel had planned to get a little apartment and to continue his Air Force career alone.

Brenda was floored. She did not see it coming. "When I had left Colorado, I thought we were happily married. Sure, we had our issues," she explained. "But isn't that how life is?"

Add to that, stresses had been building. "Apparently, my clinical depression had come back," she explained. Despite the depression, Brenda pulled herself together and came up with a plan.

First, she felt all fired up. She was angry. She thought to herself, "I basically just buried my mother, and you pull this crap on me? We didn't just spend two years, prior to the one in Colorado busting our butts getting you through college so you could have a better life just for you to dump us now that we're finally about to see the light at the end of the tunnel! I don't think so, Buster!"

Brenda was not going to take this lying down, nor would she let go of her husband and the father of her children. "So, I asked Joel to come to California so we could discuss this in person, and thankfully he agreed to do that." Reflecting on that fateful time, she said, "God had His hands all over this, of course!" She had no doubt.

"So we agreed to attend Mass together as a family." Joel had been away from the Church except when occasionally dropping the kids off at Mass, and Brenda had previously had issues with the Church and didn't attend Mass. Now, they'd go together. Eventually a very helpful deacon encouraged Brenda to take part in the RCIA program so that she could understand the Catholic Faith.

Brenda attended counseling sessions for her depression and started on an antidepressant. They chose a military-base chapel for their parish. Everything came together for this family by the grace of God. Joel finished his Sacraments of Initiation by making his Confirmation, and Brenda has been "attending adult faith-formation classes, conferences, workshops, and retreats to learn more about this wonderful gift God has given us called the Catholic Church." Brenda is grateful for God's blessings in her life. "I thank God all the time for His patience with me and continuing to call me to Him until I finally let Him into my heart and marriage. I believe that's what saved our marriage when we were at our lowest point."

Reflecting on her journey, Brenda notes, "Joel and I would have very different lives if it weren't for God's graces and blessings." She adds, "A lot of military couples don't seem to know how to put God into their marriage so that they have the strength to stay together when things get tough."

Lean on the Cross of Christ
St. Anthony of Padua (1195–1231)

Christians must lean on the Cross of Christ
just as travelers lean on a staff
when they begin a journey.
They must have the Passion of Christ
deeply embedded in their minds and hearts,
because only from it can they
derive peace, grace, and truth.

By Dawn's Early Light

Prayer for Protection for
My Soldier and Our Family

Dear Lord Jesus,
please protect my soldier and our family.
We are riddled with stress and strains,
trying to get through each day.
We are at times in the dark with all the unseen
physical, emotional, and mental effects of war.
We cannot see into the future,
but want to make sure it ends up with You.
Please protect us and continue to guide us
each day, placing people in our lives
to help us and people for us to help.
Jesus, we trust in You! Amen.

Walking in the Dark

In my memoir, *The Kiss of Jesus,* in the section titled "Serving God in Darkness and Trial," I wrote:

> St. Thérèse of Lisieux also wrote: "It is good to serve God in darkness and trial! We have only this life to live by faith." Walking in faith sometimes seems like walking in the dark. I seemed to grope blindly a lot throughout my life, but with a certainty, or at least a strong hope, that there would be light—somewhere. I needed to trust God fully with my life, and I prayed to do so. When I found myself in darkness I continued to search for God there, and I strove to serve him each day in the people he put around me, starting in my own family.
>
> Mother Teresa's example of carrying a light of faith to others through the darkness resonated in my heart. God grants us the graces not merely to grope and to struggle through the darkness, but to be a reflection of Christ's light to others even as we endure suffering and pain in our darkness.[20]

The Kiss of Jesus

St. Teresa of Calcutta, someone I still often call Mother Teresa because she was such a mother to me, taught me many lessons in the time I knew her. But she continues to teach me long after she has gone to her eternal reward. I have no doubt that she is working even harder in Heaven than she did when she worked

[20] Cooper O'Boyle, *The Kiss of Jesus,* 116.

tirelessly in the slums of Calcutta. But now she is also beholding the Face of Christ. Imagine that!

Mother Teresa knew of the suffering in my life. I had shared it very openly with her, and she prayed for me. One of the most poignant and powerful things she told me was that Jesus loved me and had allowed me to come close to His Cross. She specifically told me, "Suffering is a sharing in the Passion of Christ. Suffering is the kiss of Jesus, a sign that you have come so close to Jesus on the Cross that He can kiss you. Do offer some of your sufferings for us and our people." Her words moved me intensely, and I am so happy to share them with the world in the hope of helping to bring meaning to others' sufferings.

In her book *Life in the Spirit*, Mother Teresa wrote:

> Today the world is an "open Calvary." Mental and physical suffering is everywhere. Pain and suffering have to come into your life.... Accept them as a gift—all for Jesus. You are reliving the passion of Christ so accept Jesus as he comes into your life—bruised, divided, full of pains and wounds.... Suffering in itself is nothing: but suffering shared with Christ's passion is a wonderful gift.[21]

Mother Teresa goes on to say some seemingly contradictory words: "Suffering, if it is accepted together, borne together, is joy." Joy? See what I mean by "contradictory"? But, Mother Teresa reminds us:

> Remember that the passion of Christ ends always in the joy of the resurrection of Christ, so when you feel in your

---

[21] Mother Teresa and Kathryn Spink, *Life in the Spirit: Reflections, Meditations, Prayers*, 1st U.S. ed. (San Francisco: Harper and Row, 1983), 62.

own heart the suffering of Christ, remember the resurrection has to come — the joy of Easter has to dawn. Never let anything so fill you with sorrow as to make you forget the joy of the risen Christ.[22]

The Children Are Affected

Marine wife Linda Bontempo Coleman entered military life because, as she puts it, "I fell in love with my Marine!" It turns out that, before she courted her future husband, his youngest sister, who was one of Linda's students, felt a need to play matchmaker. The clincher was when this well-meaning student showed Linda a photo of her big brother Larry in his Dress Blues. Linda shared, "If you have ever seen a photo of a Marine in his Dress Blues, you will understand!"

Linda and her Marine courted and were happily married in the church where Linda grew up, and they went on to have five children. Larry has served more than twenty-four years on active duty thus far. Linda stays connected with other military wives and her family as well. She remains grounded in her Faith through a variety of activities and clubs, including the CWOC and the MCCW-Worldwide. She says she keeps her sanity with "coffee, chocolate, prayer, Mass, coffee, wine, walking my dog, chocolate, coffee, talking with my younger sister, talking to Mom." Possibly, not all in that order! Perhaps in moderation — or not! Linda smiled and added, "Let's not forget about the occasional Ladies Night Out or coffee! Those feed my soul as well as my body!"

[22] Ibid., 63.

By Dawn's Early Light

Reflecting on how her children are affected by military life, Linda said, "Children are affected by the frequent moving, the absence of the military parent, and the aftermath of post-traumatic stress disorder." Linda pointed out that not all the problems are apparent or even visible. She explained, "One of the major issues affecting service members, veterans, and their families is the long-lasting impact of both visible and invisible wounds. The stress experienced by a child of a service member is often overlooked. These children face challenges and adversities that someone their age should not have to handle."

On the bright side, though, there are beneficial traits that the children learn when living in a military family. Linda explained, "Military children learn to be resilient. They learn to make new friends no matter where they are." This is a necessity, given the amount of moving they do. Linda observed that because of their unique lives, "I believe military kids learn to try new things. They learn that change is a part of life, but that there are consistencies even within the change.

"Thank God for our Faith!" No matter what the situation, "our faith and trust in God doesn't change," Linda points out. "My children have learned that there are Catholic churches *everywhere*—sometimes you just have to look a little harder to find one, but you can always find a Mass if you can access the Internet!"

Prayer to Christ Crucified

Behold, O good and sweetest Jesus,
I cast myself upon my knees in Thy sight,
and with the most fervent desire of my soul

Take Up Your Cross

I pray and beseech Thee
to impress upon my heart
lively sentiments of faith, hope, and charity,
with true repentance for my sins
and a most firm desire of amendment,
whilst with deep affection and grief of soul
I consider within myself and mentally contemplate
Thy five most precious wounds,
having before mine eyes that which
David, the prophet, long ago spoke
in Thine own person
concerning Thee, my Jesus:
They have pierced my hands and my feet,
they have numbered all my bones. Amen.

Reflection on the Cross
Archbishop Fulton Sheen (1895–1979)

Everyone who suffers is on a cross.
Some ask to be taken down,
like the thief on the left.
Others want to be taken up,
like the thief on the right.[23]

---

[23] *Fulton Sheen's Wartime Prayer Book*, 37–38.

By Dawn's Early Light

Pruning and Growing

There are times in life when we undergo more suffering than not. We might wonder why. We might even think it's not fair and rebel against it. A couple of times a year, I take my pruning tools out of the shed. I go around my yard and clip and prune the dead branches off the trees and shrubs. My mother had taught me that it's best to cut the dead parts off a plant so that it doesn't exert energy trying to fix those dead parts of itself. When the bad or dead parts are pruned away, the plant can blossom more beautifully and produce more bountifully.

Our Lord Jesus has told us, "I am the true vine, and my Father is the vine grower. He removes every branch in me that bears no fruit. Every branch that bears fruit he prunes to make it bear more fruit" (John 15:1–2). When we feel the pinch here and there or the desolation, we can turn to Jesus and know that He is working on us. He'll give us every grace we need. We should be patient with the process and continue to pray to grow and blossom in the Faith.

Fulton Sheen, who was no stranger to intense suffering, assures us of the need for pruning and the beautiful surprise of the harvest. He said:

> Our Blessed Lord used a powerful simile when he talked to his apostles the night of the Last Supper.... So the heavenly Father purges us. A discipline, a trial, a handicap, or a cross comes into our life. And why is the pruning done? To make us more fruitful. That's why we've asked for this change, for more fruit. Our vines must be pruned. We will be surprised at the richness of the harvest.[24]

[24] Fulton J. Sheen and Henry Dieterich, *Through the Year with Fulton Sheen* (San Francisco: Ignatius Press, 2003), 49.

Pruning Prayer

Lord, please shape my life in such a way
that it is an offering fit to finally one day
be presented before You
at the hour of my death.

I might not fully understand now
during some of the deep valleys
and dark corners of my life
that You are burnishing,
pruning, and helping me
to live my Purgatory now, dear Lord.

Please sustain me with Your grace
throughout my trials.
I give glory and praise to Your name! Amen.

In Union with Mother Mary
at the Foot of the Cross

We must always possess hope in our hearts. At Baptism we were gifted with the theological virtues of faith, hope, and love. We need to use these virtues on a regular basis and let them grow in our hearts—not let them become stagnant. St. John Paul II reminds us about Mary standing strong at the foot of her Son's Cross and how she endured great pain being united to her Son. She watched every moment of His great suffering, saw every drop of Precious Blood shed, and heard the insults, sadly even from those He had helped. St. John Paul II reminds us of great hope during our own sufferings when he says:

> The Blessed Virgin's "standing erect" at the foot of the Cross recalls her unfailing constancy and extraordinary courage in facing suffering. In the tragic events of Calvary, Mary is sustained by faith, strengthened during the events of her life and especially during Jesus' public life. The [Second Vatican] Council reminds us that "the Blessed Virgin advanced in her pilgrimage of faith and faithfully persevered in her union with her Son unto the Cross."[25]
>
> Sharing his deepest feelings, she counters the arrogant insults addressed to the crucified Messiah with forbearance and pardon, associating herself with his prayer to the Father: "Forgive them, for they know not what they do" (Luke 23:34). By sharing in the feeling of abandonment to the Father's will expressed in Jesus' last

---

[25] Second Vatican Council, Dogmatic Constitution on the Church *Lumen Gentium* (November 21, 1964), no. 58.

words on the Cross: "Father into your hands I commend my spirit!" (Luke 23:46), she thus offers, as the Council notes, loving consent "to the immolation of this victim which was born of her."[26] Mary's hope at the foot of the Cross contains a light stronger than the darkness that reigns in many hearts: in the presence of the redeeming Sacrifice, the hope of the Church and of humanity is born in Mary.[27]

We can turn to Mother Mary at any time and especially when enduring the crosses of life. She is sure to offer us unending hope and grace.

---

[26] Ibid.
[27] St. John Paul II, General Audience, April 2, 1997.

God Is My Strength and My Salvation

Jesus says, "If any want to become my followers, let them deny themselves and take up their cross and follow me" (Matt. 16:24). To be a true Christian requires sacrificial love. By staying close to Jesus, Mary, the saints and angels, we will be sustained in our sufferings and more able to lovingly offer them to Jesus so that he can transform them into beautiful graces for ourselves and others.

Prayer to Jesus

You alone know my heart, O Lord.
You are the Divine Physician
and know exactly what I need
and when I need it.
Please grant me the graces to continue
to pick up my cross and follow You.
Help me to be more generous with my time
in helping to bring others to You.
Jesus, I trust in You! Amen.

4

Be Countercultural

Do not be conformed to this world, but be transformed by the renewing of your minds, so that you may discern what is the will of God—what is good and acceptable and perfect.

—Romans 12:2

I love Archbishop Fulton Sheen's encouragement to the faithful to lead countercultural lives. He told us not to be a "dead body"! That's right—a dead body. Specifically, he wrote:

> Thirty or forty years ago it was easy to be a Christian. The very air we breathed was Christian. Bicycles could be left on front lawns; doors could be left unlocked. Suddenly, all this has changed. Now we have to affirm our faith. We live in a world that challenges us. And many fall away. Dead bodies float downstream; it takes live bodies to resist the current. And this is our summons.[28]

Family Life in the "Village"

In my books and talks, I often warn parents and grandparents to beware of our culture, which continually bombards us with many allurements that are directly opposed to our Christianity. In fact, in my book *Embracing Motherhood*, I spoke about that adage "It takes a village to raise a child":

> I recognize that a faithful Catholic mother should never want her "village" (society or government) to raise her child, at least not today! We know all too well what is

---

[28] Sheen and Dieterich, *Through the Year with Fulton Sheen*, 28.

happening around us in our world, much of it precisely what we want to keep our children away from. Our culture doesn't share our values—we don't want to set our kids free on the streets of New York City any time soon, or even in the woods where I live in New England. The closely-knit community in Africa where this familiar proverb evidently originated is not necessarily like what we experience in our own neighborhoods—and certainly not in the larger culture.

As idyllic as the phrase sounds, mothers need to be very careful when it comes to entrusting the care of their children to others. We mustn't be naive. Just think what could have happened if Mary and Joseph allowed the village to raise Jesus.[29]

I learned about another kind of "village," however, when I came to know military women. They have a loving "village" helping them to raise their children. Military families are required to move their families often—to get up and go! They often connect with brand-new neighbors at a military base, people they hardly know, and come to depend on them and seek their help in emergencies and at other times.

Being part of the military means a lot to military wife Kelly Oliver. She described to me the various factors of military life: "Military life is exciting, challenging, lonely, fulfilling, and definitely unique!" Kelly is married to Jeff, a Lieutenant Colonel in the Army, whose father served in World War II and Korea and whose brothers served in Vietnam and Germany. Kelly believes

---

[29] Donna-Marie Cooper O'Boyle, *Embracing Motherhood: A Vocation of Love* (Cincinnati: Servant Books, 2012), 53–54.

that "military life is as unique and diverse as its people; the common denominator is the sense of community and pride for our country." She added, "As military families, we serve together in unity."

Kelly joyfully shared, "I am humbled and proud that my husband is a soldier, and I always cry at the National Anthem and Taps, for I know what every note means." Kelly, who is actively involved with the MCCW and the CWOC, also volunteers in her children's schools and participates in military spouse clubs. She shared with me that her family had a chance to assist at their new "village," by pitching in to help right after they moved in. It was at a time when most of the families at the post had a loved one who was deployed and they were feeling weary. Kelly's husband had just returned from a deployment from a previous duty station and wouldn't be deploying anytime soon. Even though they were brand new at the post, Kelly said that Jeff and the children "had an opportunity to minister with our time and talents to many families. My teenagers babysat neighbor children so the moms would have a little 'me time.' I had the opportunity to help cook, run errands, and encourage many families. We made ourselves available. I believe God sent us there to serve and offer hope. It was a blessed time for all of us," she joyfully explained.

Air Force wife Aimee Miller loves the community aspect of the military. She said she got involved in military life because of "love": she married into it. She told me, "The greatest help to me about military life is the sense of community, finding new friends, and making them my 'station family.' For example, we had our Germany family, and now we have our Idaho family. These are friends who are very dear and close to us." Aimee went on about her experience in what I affectionately call "the military village": "They will watch my children when I have a baby, or when I need to take one to the ER and my husband is deployed." She says these are the ones who "will bring me wine or let me cry on their shoulders." What can be kinder than that? These women become "soul sisters" looking out for one another and their families.

Aimee has been involved in the military for more than fifteen years. She is a member of a unit spouses group and the Mom-2Mom breastfeeding support group. She has also been involved with the MCCW and the CWOC.

As much as Aimee is thankful for "an amazing support network in the Catholic community" which helps to bolster her faith, she and her family have experienced many challenges. One challenge stands out in her mind: "I think moving is harder than a deployment." She said there is so much to it. "Purging. Packing up your whole life. Cleaning your house while children have nothing to do. Trying to find a place to live when you are in a new country," she lamented. And there's much more. "Flying for many hours with tired children. Packing suitcases for warm weather and chilly weather." She explained, "We homeschool, so we had to throw schoolbooks into suitcases as well." The list goes on. "Sleeping on air mattresses that children often pop. Repurchasing all the essentials for your pantry. Finding a new parish. Finding where you belong. Making new friends. Plus, so much more," she adds. "The logistics behind these massive moves are great. You do it, and make it work, but it's definitely the most challenging thing to me," she said.

Be Countercultural

Prayer to St. Joseph

St. Joseph, you are the chaste
and loving spouse
of the Virgin Mary,
the foster father of Jesus,
the provider and protector
of the Holy Family and of all families.
We have complete confidence
in your loving care for new life
and in your fidelity to the family.
Despise not our prayer,
but graciously hear us. Amen.

---------------- ☆ ----------------

Strengthen Our Families, Lord!

Please give us strength, dear Lord.
Sometimes we lose our way.
Many times we are weary because
of all we are required to do.
Each day has its share of
difficult challenges and splendid joys.
Help me to embrace it
for all it's worth and to strive
wholeheartedly always to follow You. Amen.

Strengthening One Another

Faith-filled military women seek to strengthen one another. They join church groups at their bases, such as the Catholic Women of the Chapel group and the worldwide Military Council of Catholic Women. They share their faith in many ways. They understand the plight of military families and want the best for one another. Like Kelly Oliver and her family, whom I mentioned earlier, and countless other military women and their families, if they can help to lift any stress or strain from another, they'll be right there to do so. Their heroism doesn't remain on the battlefield—it is woven into the very fabric of their lives.

Air Force wife Brenda Nonnweiler shared with me how, in the military, Christian women come together to nourish their faith and one another. She said, "Ideally, when we come together regularly to share, learn more about, and celebrate our faith with one another, we can support each other in our daily lives and struggles." She added, "When we share experiences and learn more about each other as we share our love of Christ with each other, we can nurture one another and help each other grow in faith as well as other aspects of our lives." Brenda feels passionate about their need to stand by one another. "We should be standing together and encouraging one another and our families," she said, "because if we don't encourage each other, who will?" She explained that it is difficult for others to understand what military families live through and what they are up against on any given day. "Who knows our struggles better than other women going through the same things we are going through?" she added. That's why these amazing women become so close and rely on one another for strength—that is, after God, from whom they derive their true strength and grace. Their military sisters are a beautiful reflection of God's love.

"Being there for one another is so important," said Army wife Kim Miller. It's only natural at times to feel a certain hesitancy about speaking up in some situations when you fear you might say the wrong thing and make a person feel even worse. However, Kim explains from experience, "When someone, a dear friend or just a casual acquaintance, is going through a difficult time, it can be easy to think, 'I don't know the right thing to say or do, so I am just going to do nothing, because I don't want to do the wrong thing.'" Yet Kim wholeheartedly believes that "it is far better not to worry about getting it right and just be there for that person." It's pivotal to help a person experiencing a loss or deep challenges to know that he or she is not alone. Kim shares, "This life has a lot of unique challenges, and we all need to know that we aren't alone and that we can find our way through the tough times together." She also explained what she does and how she prays when she is unsure of what to say or do. "In uncertain situations these days, I usually just pray, 'God, you take the lead. Give me whatever graces I need in this situation,' and I find that I can move forward and be there."

Help Me to Help, Lord

Dear Lord Jesus,
please help me to be open
to Your love and prodding
to reach forth and help
my fellow military sister in Christ.

By Dawn's Early Light

Please live in me and shine through me
so that Your great love may be radiated
through my loving actions to help others.
Thank You for Your abiding love.
I love You! Amen.

Dear Holy Family

Dear Holy Family of Nazareth,
please assist my family
during all our moves,
and in our daily struggles.
In all deployments, keep us safe.
Inspire us to be a constant help
and encouragement
to all those in our
military family and beyond.
Jesus, Mary, and Joseph,
stay with us please. Amen.

Prayer for the Seven Gifts of the Holy Spirit
St. Alphonsus Liguori (1696–1787)

Holy Spirit, Divine Consoler,
I adore You as my true God,
with God the Father and God the Son.

Be Countercultural

I adore You and unite myself to the adoration
You receive from the angels and saints.

I give You my heart, and I offer
my ardent thanksgiving for all the grace
that You never cease to bestow on me.

O giver of all supernatural gifts,
who filled the soul of the Blessed Virgin Mary,
Mother of God, with such immense favors,
I beg You to visit me with Your grace and Your love.

Grant me the gift of *holy fear*,
so that it may act on me as a check
to prevent me from falling back
into my past sins, for which I beg pardon.

Grant me the gift of *piety*,
so that I may serve You
for the future with increased fervor,
follow with more promptness
Your holy inspirations, and observe
Your divine precepts with greater fidelity.

Grant me the gift of *knowledge*,
so that I may know the things of God and,
enlightened by Your holy teaching,
may walk, without deviation,
in the path of eternal salvation.

Grant me the gift of *fortitude*,
so that I may overcome courageously
all the assaults of the devil,
and all the dangers of this world that

By Dawn's Early Light

threaten the salvation of my soul.

Grant me the gift of *counsel*,
so that I may choose what is more
conducive to my spiritual advancement
and may discover the wiles
and snares of the tempter.

Grant me the gift of *understanding*,
so that I may apprehend the divine mysteries
and by contemplation of heavenly things detach
my thoughts and affections from the vain things
of this miserable world.

Grant me the gift of *wisdom*,
so that I may rightly direct all my actions,
referring them to God as my last end;
so that, having loved You and served You
in this life, I may have the happiness of
possessing You eternally in the next. Amen.

Keeping It Real Amid Struggle

Army wife Karen Smith got involved in military life "only because I was so in love with a man who made the commitment to
serve." She explained, "He didn't ever imagine making a career
of the military!" Karen believes that the military "will stretch and
strengthen you in ways you'd never imagine." She said that the
constant changes in military life are indeed challenging, but they
"have made me resilient and adaptable, proud, and confident."
When it comes to the kids, she exuberantly shared, "I teach my
kids that life is a creative problem-solving adventure!"

Karen grew up on Aquidneck Island, Rhode Island, and rarely
left it for the first twenty-one years of her life. The military has
expanded her horizons in numerous ways, one being the places
she has traveled, which she had previously only dreamed about,
as well as the places she has lived, such as Korea, Kuwait, Germany, and all over the continental United States.

She is amazed at how her life has changed throughout the
years of zigging and zagging—physically through relocations
and even emotionally and spiritually. And to think that she
used to imagine that the sun exclusively rose and set on her
island of Aquidneck. "I thought that all I wanted in life was to
live on my island, marry a boy named Sullivan or Murphy, and
compete with the natives." As Karen reflected on the unique-
ness of military life, she said, "I am so profoundly grateful for the
opportunities of exposure and enlightenment that the military
has allowed me."

Karen is also deeply thankful for a most poignant piece of
advice that she and her husband received early in his military
career. She shared, "A priest told us that no matter who you
are—a four-star general who is retiring, a captain who is being

passed over for promotion, or a junior soldier who is being thrown out for being overweight, you must define yourself away from the Army." She said it was "the best advice ever." Military personnel and their families should not see the military as their entire universe, according to the wise priest friend. "Unfortunately," Karen noted, "it is the case for many, many people" who view and define themselves as military. "Spouses are especially susceptible to this," she added. "Defining themselves by their husbands' rank and status."

Karen courageously and openly shared about a very dark and trying experience brought on by the stresses and strains of military life. When her husband was deployed to Romania when the family lived in Heidelberg, Germany, she began to drink to excess. "I was drinking regularly to relax and escape the stress" she explained. At that time, Karen's twelve-year-old son was having some trouble in school and her four-year-old daughter began to act out in tantrums. Dad came home for four months and was off again—this time to Afghanistan for a year.

The family took on a routine of "lots of sports, religious education, school activities, and music lessons" recalled Karen. Each day they were home early, so the youngest could get to bed and Karen would drink herself "into a stupor while the boys looked after themselves."

There was not an awful lot that would give Karen a reason to smile or laugh. Yes, her children were the light of her life, but she was in survival mode. Yet, a time of laughing was just around the corner. This stressed-out Army wife would meet a supportive friend at work at the chapel.

"He adored me and made me laugh," she recalled. "Had I not been drinking, I would've seen this coming a mile away!" She was blind to what was happening. Her need for affirmation took precedence. She learned the hard way that "they call him Lucifer for a reason. He always comes carrying a light," as her beloved priest friend would later tell her when she sought his help. Before realizing or allowing herself to recognize what she was getting into, Karen was placing all of her thoughts and energy into texting and calling this new friend to set up meetings with him whenever possible.

"What a mess," she confessed to me. "My son now had a double vacuum to fill. Even though I was showing up as the perfect mom and military wife, I was completely checked out," Karen recalled. "All around, people saw us as the ultimate in resilient, thriving military families, and had no idea of the truth."

She later confessed everything to her husband, whom she calls "an amazing man." But, she said, "my teenage boys both found out about it, and it was ugly." By God's amazing grace, the family worked through their difficulties. "Time and evidence of change has healed things with my boys," Karen told me. Counseling became a lifesaver. Alcoholics Anonymous was a Godsend. "I walked into my first AA meeting with my husband by my side about four months after his return from Afghanistan," Karen shared. "God brought me to AA, and AA brought me to God! Best thing ever!" she exclaimed.

God Calls Us to Himself

Over the years, Karen and her husband tried to keep in mind the important advice their priest friend gave them, and they did their best to navigate their ever-changing military lives, being constantly uprooted and sometimes disappointed, particularly over Karen's husband's being "passed over for promotion" after several years, feeling humiliated, depressed, going through various dark times, and so much more. Later, though, there were triumphs. Karen's husband stuck it out when he was seriously thinking of jumping ship and resigning from the Army. One superior encouraged him to hang in there. Just a year after being passed over, Karen's husband was made Major and received orders to go to Korea with his family. It was in Korea that God gifted this family with a beautiful baby girl who stole their hearts when they were delivering gifts to a local orphanage. Karen shared that many miracles were involved in the process of the wee one's becoming a part of their family.

"She's been the light of our lives ever since. We then realized God's real plan!" After twenty-nine years (and counting!), Karen can honestly say that she is thankful for her military life and that she sees it "as the means by which God has brought us to Himself. The military has repeatedly put us in situations where we *needed* Christ and where we *experienced* Christ through military chapel communities."

Prayer for Stability, Balance, and Sanity

Dear Lord, Jesus, please help me to remain balanced and to make wise and prudent decisions each and every day. Shield me from the evil influences of the world. Strengthen my resolve. Help me to hang in here with my responsibilities and not to jump ship when things are tough. Thank You, dear Lord for Your great love for me. Amen.

Taking Off the Masks

Army wife Karen believes that "military wives wear masks all the time." Perhaps some do so without realizing it. Some might hide behind the rank and status of their husbands. Others are intimidated or frightened by things beyond their power.

Karen has also experienced resentment aimed at her due to her husband's rank. She had taken on duties as part of a command team to help families, provide support for young spouses, plan activities and circulate information to those in her husband's command. She explained, "There is an age-old gap between officer and enlisted spouses that takes on a life of its own when you put yourself out there. There is a resentment some women feel, and they let me know when I let something slip!"

Karen has found help in sharing with trusted friends. She participates in a morning Bible-study group. "The women are so genuine and tolerant. . . . This group creates a safe place to drop those masks." During their get-togethers, they share their "struggles and triumphs and cheer each other on as we journey with Christ." Karen loves that, while sharing together, "no one personality or point-of-view dominates."

"I love to experience God in a group of believers," Karen told me. To bolster their faith and feel connected to other faith-filled women, military women all over can come together to study their faith and share their hearts, confiding in one another in a safe environment and experiencing wonderful Christian camaraderie.

By Dawn's Early Light

Conversion of Heart

Jesus' call to conversion and penance, like that of the prophets before him, does not aim first at outward works, "sackcloth and ashes," fasting and mortification, but at *conversion of the heart: interior conversion.* Without this, penances remain sterile and false; however, interior conversion urges expression in visible signs, gestures, and works of penance (cf. Joel 2:12–13; Isa. 1:16–17; Matt. 6:1–6; 16–18).

Interior repentance is a radical reorientation of our whole life, a return, a conversion to God with all our heart, an end of sin, a turning away from evil, with repugnance toward the evil actions we have committed. At the same time, it entails the desire and resolution to change one's life, with hope in God's mercy and trust in the help of his grace.[30] (CCC 1430–1431)

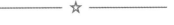

Take My Mask, Lord

Take my mask, Lord.
Help me to reach out
in utter simplicity, peace, and love
to my fellow military sisters in Christ.
Help me to trust in Your everlasting love
and mercy for us all. Amen.

---

[30] Cf. Council of Trent (1551): DS 1676–1678; 1705; cf. *Roman Catechism*, II, V, 4.

Prayer for Those We Love
St. Ambrose of Milan (340–397)

Lord God, we can hope for others nothing better
than the happiness we desire for ourselves.
Therefore, I pray You, do not separate me
after death from those I tenderly loved on earth.
Grant that where I am they may be with me,
and that I may enjoy their presence in Heaven
after being so often deprived of it on earth.
Lord God, I ask You to receive Your beloved children
immediately into Your life-giving heart.
After this brief life on earth,
give them eternal happiness. Amen.

God Is My Strength and My Salvation

God calls us to renewal. "Do not be conformed to this world, but be transformed by the renewing of your minds, so that you may discern what is the will of God—what is good and acceptable and perfect" (Rom. 12:2). We certainly don't want to be a "dead body" floating downstream, such as the Servant of God Fulton Sheen warned us about! We need to lead countercultural lives and be a light to others. God is counting on us.

Prayer to Mother Mary

Dear Mother Mary, please bring me closer to your Son Jesus. Grant me the graces to be more virtuous each day and to help guide others to do the same—starting within my own family and then reaching out to my military family and beyond.

O, Mary, conceived without sin, pray for us who have recourse to thee. Amen.

Part 2

True Stories of Behind-the-Scenes Service

Behold, I am the handmaid of the Lord.
May it be done to me according to your word.

—Luke 1:38

5

Be Humble

Femininity has a unique relationship with the mother of the Redeemer. . . . The figure of Mary of Nazareth sheds light on womanhood as such by the very fact that God, in the sublime event of the Incarnation of his Son, entrusted Himself to the ministry, the free and active ministry of a woman.

—St. John Paul II, *Redemptoris Mater*, no. 46

In a beautiful act of love, the Blessed Virgin Mary gave her fiat or, yes, at the Annunciation, when the angel Gabriel announced to her that she would be overshadowed by the Holy Spirit and would become the Mother of God. Again, at the foot of the Cross, Mary gave her fiat when Jesus gave us the eminent gift of His Mother.

St. John Paul II encouraged us to call upon Mother Mary in all of our needs and to ask her to be a companion on our pilgrimage through life. He said, "This woman of faith, Mary of Nazareth, the mother of God, has been given to us as a model in our pilgrimage of faith." We would learn so much from Mary if only we would pause in our busy lives to listen and learn: "From Mary we learn to surrender to God's will in all things. From Mary we learn to trust even when all hope seems gone. From Mary we learn to love Christ, her Son and the Son of God. For Mary is not only the mother of God, she is the mother of the Church as well." St. John Paul II also reminded the faithful that throughout history the Church has been protected and blessed by Mary. Specifically, he said, "In every stage of the march through history, the Church has benefited from the prayer and protection of the Virgin Mary.... Mary appears particularly close to the Church, because for her the Church is always her beloved Christ."[31]

---

[31] Pope John Paul II and Margaret Bunson, *John Paul II's Book of Mary* (Huntington, IN.: Our Sunday Visitor, 1996), 140.

By Dawn's Early Light

During a General Audience, the pontiff pointed out that Mary's participation with her Son Jesus spanned His entire life, beginning at the Annunciation by the angel Gabriel and culminating at the Cross at Jesus' death. He said:

> In accepting with complete availability the words of the angel Gabriel, who announced to her that she would become the mother of the Messiah, Mary began her participation in the drama of Redemption. Her involvement in her Son's sacrifice, revealed by Simeon during the presentation in the Temple, continues not only in the episode of the losing and finding of the 12-year-old Jesus, but also throughout his public life.
>
> However, the Blessed Virgin's association with Christ's mission reaches its culmination in Jerusalem, at the time of the Redeemer's Passion and Death.... The [Second Vatican] Council text also stresses that her consent to Jesus' immolation is not passive acceptance but a genuine act of love, by which she offers her Son as a "victim" of expiation for the sins of all humanity.[32]

Mary Is Our True Mother

Mary is our true Mother. We shouldn't fear getting to know her or think of her as some unreachable saint of ages past or so far away. She is with us and wants to mother us. We might also fear that she couldn't possibly have anything in common with us because she was, after all, the Mother of God! But, we must remember that she was human like us and needed to be steadfast

[32] St. John Paul II, General Audience, April 2, 1997.

in her faith and in her prayers. She knew and still knows all about life's challenges and suffering. We are so blessed to be given the gift of the Mother of God! We will never fathom the full meaning of it until we get to Heaven. It was Jesus, as He was dying on the Cross, who gave us the eminent gift of His own Mother: "Here is your mother" (John 19:27).

John the Baptist jumped in the womb of his mother, St. Elizabeth, when he heard Mary's holy and soothing voice (Luke 1:44). The presence of Mary and the unborn Jesus certainly touched Elizabeth's heart in a profound way—and even her unborn son, John the Baptist! Mary is sure to comfort us in all our needs. Let's be sure to draw near to her in our prayers.

Mary's Spiritual Motherhood

Throughout the years of raising Jesus, Mary's motherly heart went out to her beloved Son, but she also impacted others who were close to her, such as dear St. Joseph, their neighbors, and those she knew at the synagogue, as well as those who had asked for her prayers. We can be sure that in Mary's quiet, humble, holy way, she made a great difference in the lives of others, always directing them to her Son Jesus.

In John's Gospel we read, "Standing by the cross of Jesus was his mother" (John 19:25). We know that Mary never deserted her Son and was always joined with Him throughout salvation history—all the way to the Cross and beyond—and is still working hard from Heaven to rescue souls. Our Lord God in Heaven sustained the Virgin Mary with courage and faith to stand beneath the Cross of her Son.

Fulton Sheen explained how Mary's spiritual motherhood came about. He said, "Mary was destined to have other children than Jesus, but they were to be born not of her flesh but of her heart." He went on to explain that Mary's firstborn was brought into the world in great joy, but that, because of Eve's sin, her future children were brought forth at the Cross, where Mary, in a sense, birthed her spiritual children in sorrow. "At that moment Mary suffered the pangs of childbirth for the millions of souls who would ever be called to adoptive sonship of the Father, to brotherhood of Christ, and to the joy of calling her mother."[33]

St. John Paul II reminds us of Mother Mary's role as a co-redeemer with our Lord Jesus. He said, "Mary, the mother of the Redeemer, constantly remained beside Christ in his journey toward the human family and in its midst, and she goes before the Church on the pilgrimage of faith."[34]

On May 13, 1982, at Fatima, Portugal, St. John Paul II consecrated the world to the Immaculate Heart of Mary. He talked about the union of Mary's Immaculate Heart and Jesus' pierced Heart and their love for mankind. He noted how Jesus' words on the Cross opened Mary's heart to a new and profound role. He said:

> On the cross Christ said: "Woman, behold your son!" With these words he opened in a new way his mother's heart. A little later, the Roman soldier's spear pierced the side of the Crucified One. That pierced heart became a sign of the Redemption achieved through the death of the Lamb of God.
>
> The Immaculate Heart of Mary—opened with the words "Woman, behold, your son!"—is spiritually united with the heart of her Son, opened by the same love for

[33] *Fulton Sheen's Wartime Prayer Book*, 92.
[34] St. John Paul II, Encyclical Letter *Centesimus Annus* (May 1, 1991), no. 62.

man and for the world with which Christ loved man and the world, offering himself for them on the cross, until the soldier's spear struck that blow.

Consecrating the world to the Immaculate Heart of Mary means drawing near, through the mother's intercession, to the very Fountain of Life that sprang from Golgotha. This Fountain pours forth unceasingly redemption and grace. In it reparation is made consensually for the sins of the world. It is a ceaseless source of new life and holiness.

In addition to the fact that the Blessed Mother, Queen of Heaven and Earth, has been bequeathed to us as an eminent gift from her own Son as he was hanging on the Cross, ready to give His last breath for love of all mankind, we can also reflect upon the fact that we can endeavor to unite our own "crosses" and the "crosses" of our day, and we can ask for the necessary graces to continue to fight the good fight. Lovingly offering our sufferings and encouraging others to do so brings about amazing transformation and strength. It brings about victory! St. John Paul II wrote about this in *Christifideles Laici*. He stated:

> Together with Mary, mother of Christ, who stood beneath the cross, we pause beside all the crosses of contemporary man and we ask all of you who suffer to support us. We ask precisely you who are weak to become a source of strength for the Church and humanity. In the terrible battle between the forces of good and evil revealed to our eyes by our modern world, may your sufferings in union with the cross of Christ be victorious.[35]

[35] St. John Paul II, Post-Synodal Apostolic Exhortation *Christifideles Laici* (December 30, 1989), no. 54.

By Dawn's Early Light

The Angelus

The angel of the Lord declared unto Mary:
and she conceived of the Holy Spirit.

Hail Mary, full of grace, the Lord is with thee;
blessed art thou among women
and blessed is the fruit of thy womb, Jesus.
Holy Mary, mother of God, pray for us sinners,
now and at the hour of our death. Amen.

Behold the handmaid of the Lord:
Be it done unto me according to thy word.

Hail Mary ...

And the Word was made Flesh:
And dwelt among us.

Hail Mary ...

Pray for us, O Holy mother of God,
that we may be made worthy
of the promises of Christ.

Let us pray:

Pour forth, we beseech thee, O Lord,
Thy grace into our hearts;
that we, to whom the Incarnation
of Christ, Thy Son, was made known
by the message of an angel,
may by His Passion and Cross
be brought to the glory of His Resurrection,
through the same Christ our Lord. Amen.

Mary's Great Faith

We should pause to consider Mary's great faith. She was once a young Jewish girl who prayed along with her people for the coming of the Messiah. She remained steadfast in her faith and in her prayer life. The holy example of her parents, St. Anne and St. Joachim, helped to form her in her faith. Blessed Anne Catherine Emmerich spoke about the way in which Mary was also formed supernaturally from her infancy:

> In the moment when the newborn child lay in the arms of her holy mother Anna, I saw that at the same time the child was presented in heaven in the sight of the Most Holy Trinity, and greeted with unspeakable joy by all the heavenly host. Then I understood, that there was made known to her in a supernatural manner her whole future with all her joys and sorrows. Mary was taught infinite mysteries, and yet was and remained a child. This knowledge of hers we cannot understand, because our knowledge grows on the tree of good and evil. She knew everything in the same way as a child knows its mother's breast and that it is to drink from it. As the vision faded in which I saw the child Mary being thus taught in heaven through grace, I heard her weep for the first time.[36]

Mary's great faith did not waver even when things seemed quite impossible. We should consider what might have crossed her mind when the angel Gabriel told her that she was to become the Mother of God! Mary believed God's Word! She had faith in

[36] Blessed Anne Catherine Emmerich, *The Life of the Blessed Virgin Mary*, 4.3, https://www.ecatholic2000.com/anne/lom30.shtml.

what the angel disclosed to her even though it wasn't humanly possible. She was a virgin, after all. She asked Gabriel how it could be, because she had no husband.

St. John Paul II taught that Mary in hope believed against all hope and compared Mary's faith to Abraham's:

Just as Abraham "in hope believed against hope, that he should become the father of many nations" (cf. Rom. 4:18), so Mary, at the Annunciation, having professed her virginity ("How shall this be, since I have no husband?") believed that through the power of the Most High, by the power of the Holy Spirit, she would become the mother of God's Son in accordance with the angel's revelation: "The child to be born will be called holy, the Son of God" (Luke 1:35).[37]

The Virgin Mary Offers Succor

Servant of God Fulton Sheen attested to Mother Mary's purity and even her attitude, if I may describe it that way. He said:

Mary's purity is not a holier-than-thou purity, a stand-offish holiness that gathers up its robes lest they be stained by the sinful; nor is it a despising purity that looks down upon the impure. Rather it is a radiating purity that is no more spoiled by solicitude for the fallen than sunshine is sullied by a dirty windowpane through which it pours.[38]

[37] St. John Paul II, Encyclical Letter *Redemptoris Mater* (March 25, 1987), no. 14.
[38] *Fulton Sheen's Wartime Prayer Book*, 91.

Be Humble

Pope Emeritus Benedict XVI reassures us that Mother Mary will assist us in our many needs, provided we have confidence in her intercession, as we pray in the *Memorare*. He says:

> The tears shed at the foot of the Cross have been transformed into a smile which nothing can wipe away, even as her maternal compassion towards us remains unchanged. The intervention of the Virgin Mary in offering succor throughout history testifies to this, and does not cease to call forth, in the people of God, an unshakable confidence in her: the *Memorare* prayer expresses this sentiment very well.

The pontiff underscores Mary's love for her spiritual children. He continues:

> Mary loves each of her children, giving particular attention to those who, like her Son at the hour of his Passion, are prey to suffering; she loves them quite simply because they are her children, according to the will of Christ on the Cross.[39]

We must not forget that we are Mary's children. We can run to her for every need, in every affliction. She is waiting for us and wants to be our mother. Why not "sit on her lap" in prayer? Or ask her if you can lay your head against her Immaculate Heart. She is our mother.

[39] Pope Benedict XVI, Homily in Lourdes, France, September 15, 2008.

By Dawn's Early Light

Memorare

St. Teresa of Calcutta often prayed what she called an "Express Novena," which consisted of nine Memorares in a row for an urgent need, followed by nine more in thanksgiving, even if the prayer didn't seem to be answered yet.

Remember, O most gracious Virgin Mary,
that never was it known that
anyone who fled to thy protection,
implored thy help,
or sought thy intercession
was left unaided.

Inspired by this confidence,
I fly unto thee,
O Virgin of virgins, my mother;
to thee do I come, before thee I stand,
sinful and sorrowful.
O mother of the Word Incarnate,
despise not my petitions,
but in thy mercy,
hear and answer me. Amen.

Novena Prayer to the
Immaculate Heart of Mary

O Most Blessed Mother, heart of love, heart of mercy, ever listening, caring, consoling, hear our prayer. As your children, we implore your intercession with Jesus, your Son. Receive with understanding and compassion

the petitions we place before you today, especially …
(*mention your request*).

We are comforted in knowing that your heart is ever
open to those who ask for your prayer. We trust to your
gentle care and intercession those whom we love and
who are sick or lonely or hurting. Help all of us, Holy
Mother, to bear our burdens in this life until we may
share eternal life and peace with God forever. Amen.[40]

---

[40] Novena Prayer to the Immaculate Heart of Mary, EWTN, http://
www.ewtn.com/devotionals/heart/Im_novena.htm.

Mary, Be My Mother!

In 1529, fourteen-year-old St. Teresa of Avila asked the Blessed Mother to be a mother to her. Her earthly mother had just passed away. She recalled later in her writings, "As soon as I began to understand how great a loss I had sustained by losing her, I was very much afflicted; and so I went before an image of our Blessed Lady and besought her with many tears that she would vouchsafe to be my mother."[41] St. Teresa's heartfelt request to our Lady can spur us on to do the same. Teresa grew up to become a Carmelite nun. She died in 1582 and was canonized in 1662.

A few centuries later another saint-in-the-making made a similar request of the Mother of God. It was a nine-year-old girl, who, after losing her mother, drew a statue of the Blessed Mother close to her heart and earnestly declared, "Now, dear Blessed Mother, now you will be my mother!"[42] Her name was Catherine Labouré, affectionately known as Zoe. She later became a Daughter of Charity nun. The Blessed Mother entrusted her with the great mission of propagating the Miraculous Medal. Sister Catherine died in 1876 and was proclaimed a saint by Pope Pius XII on July 27, 1947.

Another saint who was very devoted to the Blessed Mother, St. Teresa of Calcutta, taught me this very simple prayer: "Mary, Mother of Jesus, be mother to me now." Mother Teresa taught me that beautiful prayer when I was on complete bed rest with a very precarious pregnancy. I had a heart condition and a hemorrhaged uterus. The doctor didn't think the baby would make

[41] "St. Teresa of Avila," EWTN, http://www.ewtn.com/library/mary/avila.htm.
[42] Donna-Marie Cooper O'Boyle, *The Miraculous Medal: Stories, Prayers, and Devotions* (Cincinnati: Servant Books, 2013), 4.

it much past the ten weeks' gestation when I hemorrhaged. My spiritual mother, Mother Teresa, urged me to accept the Blessed Mother as my mother, assuring me that she would help me. She wrote to me, "Do not be afraid. Just put yourself in the hands of our Blessed Mother and let her take care of you. When you are afraid or sad or troubled, just tell her so. She will prove herself a mother to you. Pray often: 'Mary, Mother of Jesus, be mother to me now.' Enclosed is a Miraculous Medal. She has done wonders for others and she will do so for you, too. Just trust and pray. I am praying for you and the baby."

That unborn baby the doctor thought would not make it is now twenty-six years old! We need Mother Mary as our mother now. We should call upon her often. She will protect us and even help us to get to Heaven.

Mother Mary certainly directs us ever closer to her Son Jesus. As we know, when a bride and groom ran out of wine at their wedding celebration, she told the wine stewards, "Do whatever he tells you" (John 2:5). Mary's words are meant for all of us.

Many of the saints have attested that no one who is devoted to Mary will be lost. She will surely help them to turn their lives around and make it to Heaven one day. Servant of God Archbishop Fulton Sheen told a sweet story about the Blessed Mother's role in getting souls to Heaven. He said, "One day as our Lord was walking through the courts of heaven, he saw some souls who seemed to have won heaven quite easily. 'Peter,' he asked, 'how did these souls gain entry into my kingdom?' Peter answered, 'Don't blame me, Lord; every time I close a door, your mother opens a window.'"[43]

---

[43] *Fulton Sheen's Wartime Prayer Book*, 88.

By Dawn's Early Light

The Miraculous Medal Is Miraculous!

When St. Catherine Labouré was a novice in the Daughters of
Charity, Mary appeared to her and told her, "Have a Medal struck
after this model. All who wear it will receive great graces; they
should wear it around the neck. Graces will abound for persons
who wear it with confidence."[44] First called the medal of the Immaculate Conception and later the Miraculous Medal, countless
miracles have come about through it.

I highly recommend that everyone who is able should wear
a blessed Miraculous Medal with confidence. The prayer on the
medal, which Mary taught, is: "O, Mary, conceived without sin,
pray for us who have recourse to thee."

Servant of God Father John Hardon, S.J., a world-renowned
theologian who was my spiritual director, told the story of how
the Miraculous Medal changed his life. I tell about it in my book
The Miraculous Medal: Stories, Prayers, and Devotions.[45]

Father Hardon said that at one point he was not the "medal-
wearing kind of guy." That is, until he saw a miracle unfold before
his eyes. When Father Hardon was a young priest, a Vincentian
priest came to visit and told the group of priests all about the
Miraculous Medal and the wonders that the Blessed Mother
performs through it. Father Hardon placed the information in
his breviary. He said he wasn't impressed with what the priest
said but decided to enroll in the Confraternity anyway.

A few months later, Father Hardon was assigned to be a chaplain at a busy hospital. He came upon a nine-year-old in a coma
from a sledding accident. The boy's skull was fractured, and he

[44] Joseph I. Dirvin, *Saint Catherine Labouré of the Miraculous Medal*
(New York: Farrar, Straus, and Cudahy, 1958), chap. 8.
[45] Cooper O'Boyle, *The Miraculous Medal*, 31.

suffered inoperable and permanent brain damage. Father knew that his job was to try to console the parents and bless the boy. Then a sudden thought popped into Father Hardon's mind. He remembered the words of the Vincentian priest, "The Miraculous Medal works!" Father Hardon thought he should test it out! It couldn't hurt. The search began for a medal and then a chain to put it on.

Finally, the hospital nuns came up with a medal and a blue ribbon. Father Hardon felt a bit silly with a blue ribbon, but he blessed the medal, put it on the boy, and began to read the prayers of the investiture. He said, "No sooner did I finish the prayer of enrolling the boy in the Confraternity of the Miraculous Medal than he opened his eyes for the first time in almost two weeks. He saw his mother and said, 'Ma, I want some ice cream.'"

Father Hardon said, "This experience so changed my life that I have not been the same since. My faith in God, faith in His power to work miracles, was strengthened beyond description." He continued, "The wonders the Blessed Mother performs, provided we believe, are extraordinary."

Let's definitely remember those key words — "provided we believe." I am convinced that our Lady wants us to push a bit beyond our comfort zone to reach out to others to bring them to her and she will bring them to her Son Jesus. One way to do so is by giving blessed Miraculous Medals to others.

A "Small" Grace

I met Army wife Elizabeth Tomlin when I gave a talk to a women's group at West Point in New York. Later, she got in touch to let me know that she was enjoying my book *The Miraculous*

Medal. Since then, I have visited with Elizabeth on a few occasions when I spoke to military women on bases and at conferences. I was also blessed to visit her at her home in El Paso, Texas, with her family and there enjoyed a wonderful conversation and a delicious homecooked meal in their dining room.

Elizabeth told me that she wears "a bracelet containing medals of the saints who are especially important to me." She went on to describe them all. "There's St. Barbara—patroness of the field artillery." Elizabeth wears that one because her husband is a field-artillery officer. St. Michael the Archangel is the next medal on her bracelet. She wears it "to protect my husband." Next on her bracelet is St. Patrick, for her son Patrick. Then comes St. Joan of Arc "because of her strength" and St. George because of her son George. Next is Our Lady of Perpetual Help "because I need her." St. Anthony is next; Elizabeth loves him because "he is the great finder." She has placed St. Francis on her bracelet "because his zeal inspires me." St. Thérèse of Lisieux is included, "because her Little Way is such a powerful witness," as is St. Elizabeth Ann Seton, "because I was named for her and born on her feast day and have always prayed for her intercession as a mother." And then there's St. Thomas More because Elizabeth is a lawyer and asks for his intercession in her work.

To complete the blessed circle of medals is the Miraculous Medal, which was given to Elizabeth by her grandmother. Whenever Elizabeth spoke of a dilemma or concern, she told me, her grandmother would notoriously ask, with very knowing eyes, "Have you consulted the Blessed Mother?"

One time, Elizabeth's husband was away at military training and Elizabeth was home with all the kids for a month. After a while, she got to feeling more than a bit weary being alone and responsible for all their care. She said that whenever she'd get a few minutes of quiet, though, she enjoyed reading about the history of the Miraculous Medal as well as modern-day Miraculous Medal stories from my book. But she told me, "While I was reading your book, I lost my Miraculous Medal. I was upset and prayed that I would find it."

During her husband's absence, Elizabeth began to feel even more exhausted and worn down from all her responsibilities. She was lonely too, and started to feel just a bit sorry for herself. At times, she didn't remember to "consult" the Blessed Mother, as her grandmother had wisely suggested to her. At other times, she indeed reached out to Mother Mary in prayer but still felt stuck.

One night, after she put the kids to bed, she couldn't shake the feeling of not being appreciated for all she did in the home, and she was also frustrated that she couldn't work outside the home. She felt too weary to cope with her feelings. It was getting late, and though Elizabeth was thoroughly exhausted, she knew that before she could attempt to relax and settle down for the night, she had to deal with the dirty dishes in the sink.

"As I pulled on my rubber gloves at about 9:30 p.m. to finish the dinner dishes, I felt something strange in the finger of the gloves. I reached in the glove and found my Miraculous Medal!" Elizabeth was ecstatic to have found her cherished Miraculous Medal, given to her by her grandmother. She also felt that she learned an important lesson that night.

"What really struck me," she said, "is the small grace I received in finding the medal." She continued to recount her experience: "Bent over the kitchen sink, tired from a busy day, and lonely," she recalled, "I was reminded that this vocation of motherhood is something I share with our Blessed Mother, and she knows the simultaneous feelings of love and fatigue that motherhood entails."

By Dawn's Early Light

Elizabeth had much to think about as she stood by her kitchen sink that evening, drinking in the miraculous graces as she prayed for strength. She gave thanks that her eyes were opened to see that she was united with Mother Mary.

"I washed those greasy dishes and prayed for the grace to get through the next day. Mother Mary, of course, provided." Elizabeth added, "Had I not been reading your book, I might not have been so aware or appreciative of the small miracle. Thank you very much for your continued ministry."

Elizabeth's words warmed my heart and I, too, gave thanks to God. What small or big grace has unfolded in your life lately? Might God be asking you to pause and ponder — to stop and reflect on His amazing presence in your life — maybe even amid the pots and pans and small details of your life? Have you "consulted" the Blessed Mother for her help and guidance in your life? Mother Mary knows our hearts thoroughly. Let's not be afraid to reach out to her.

Let us pray the prayer taught by the Virgin Mary:

Prayer Inscribed on the Miraculous Medal

O Mary,
conceived without sin,
pray for us who have
recourse to thee.

Be Humble

Prayer to Our Lady of Perpetual Help

O Mother of Perpetual Help,
grant that I may ever invoke
thy most powerful name,
which is the safeguard of the living
and the salvation of the dying.

O purest Mary,
O sweetest Mary,
let thy name henceforth
be ever on my lips.
Delay not, O Blessed Lady,
to help me whenever I call on thee,
for, in all my needs, in all my temptations,
I shall never cease to call on thee,
ever repeating thy sacred name,
Mary, Mary.

O what consolation, what sweetness,
what confidence, what emotion
fill my soul when I pronounce
thy sacred name, or even only think of thee.
I thank God for having given thee, for my good,
so sweet, so powerful, so lovely a name.

But I will not be content
with merely pronouncing thy name:
let my love for thee prompt me ever to hail thee,
Mother of Perpetual Help. Amen.[46]

[46] "Our Lady of Perpetual Help," EWTN, http://www.ewtn.com/devotionals/prayers/perpet3.htm.

By Dawn's Early Light

Consecration to the Blessed Virgin

My queen and my mother,
I give myself entirely to you
and, in proof of my affection,
I give you my eyes, my ears,
my tongue, my heart,
my whole being without reserve.
Since I am your own,
keep me and guard me
as your property and possession. Amen.

Mary's Sorrowful Heart

Facing rejection from dear St. Joseph and possible death
by stoning, taken away from your home late in pregnancy, rejected again when searching for a birthplace for
the Savior of the world. A sword of sorrow pierced your
heart when your baby was presented in the Temple.
Later on, frantically searching for your Child. Feeling
the sting of rejection when your Son was unwelcomed
by others. Finally, to watch as He suffered on Calvary
a cruel death on the Cross, He then lay dead in your
arms. Mary, you know. Pray for me, please. Amen.[47]

---

[47] Donna-Marie Cooper O'Boyle, *A Catholic Woman's Book of Prayers*
(Brewster, MA: Paraclete Press, 2017), 74.

Hail Mary

Hail Mary,
full of grace,
the Lord is with thee.
Blessed art thou among women,
and blessed is the fruit
of thy womb, Jesus.

Holy Mary,
Mother of God,
pray for us sinners now
and at the hour of our death. Amen.

By Dawn's Early Light

Pray for Us Sinners

Once, when meditating on the Hail Mary, I paused and pondered how Mother Mary prays for us sinners. I wrote:

> When we pray the Hail Mary we beseech our mother in heaven not merely to remember us sinners but to pray for us, too. It's a prayer of humility—we admit that we are sinners and we beg for prayers. And we ask this not just from anyone but from the mother of God! We can't get any better than that except by asking God himself!
>
> We know we can't get to heaven on our own merits and prayers. We absolutely need the intercession of the mother of God. If we were more earnest about praying Hail Marys and pondered them in our hearts as we prayed, we'd be enlightened by many graces and profound mysteries.
>
> At what particular time are we begging in advance for Mary's powerful assistance? We specifically ask Mother Mary's prayers for *now and at the hour of our death*. We certainly need her prayers now while we are in the thick of it, working out our salvation through the nitty-gritty details of life. Sometimes that *now* is rolling along and peachy, but many times that *now* is arduous and even painful. We absolutely need Mary, our mother in heaven, to see us through—to actually lead us through the muck and grant us the graces we need to avoid the temptations and bombardments from our ungodly culture. We need Mary now more than ever.
>
> We also need Mary at the hour of our death because we will be tempted by the devil to despair, and we will be weak, tired, and perhaps suffering immensely. Mary

will help lift our eyes and hearts to heaven. She, being so powerful over evil, will protect us sinners from the devil at the times we need protection most—now and at the hour of our death.

Let's not wait until the hour of our death to beseech our Mother Mary or just hope that she will run in to rescue us from the pits of hell at that time. Let's nurture a special friendship with her now so she can assist us in life and guide us safely to heaven.[48]

Servant of God Fulton Sheen explained Mary's role in her prayers and love for her Son Jesus and for us sinners: "Mary stood at the deathbed of the Cross. We pray in the Hail Mary: 'Holy Mary, Mother of God, pray for us sinners, now and at the hour of our death. Amen.' To whom could we better appeal for the grace of a happy death than to her who comforted her Son in his last moments on the Cross?"[49]

Running "in Haste" to "Show Up When It Matters"

In the introduction to this book, which was written on the feast of the Visitation, I mentioned the wonderful loving act of our Blessed Mother "running in haste" to help her older cousin Elizabeth, who was also pregnant. As we know, Elizabeth was expecting John the Baptist. I wholeheartedly believe that we should strive and pray to emulate the beautiful virtues that Mother Mary practiced. Many times, we too are called to "run in haste"

---

[48] Sarah A. Reinhard, ed., *Word by Word: Slowing Down with the Hail Mary* (Notre Dame, IN: Ave Maria Press, 2015), 110–111.
[49] *Fulton Sheen's Wartime Prayer Book*, 89.

in various situations in life. Our Lord calls us to possess loving hearts that seek to serve.

Military women often run in haste to serve their fellow sisters in Christ. Army wife Elizabeth Tomlin reflected, "The friends I have met in MCCW are my best and lifelong friends. We take care of each other." She explained that military women of faith help to strengthen and serve one another. Specifically, Elizabeth recalled a time when an unexpected dish of love was delivered to her front door. She said, "One of the kindest things someone ever did for me was that a woman I barely knew sent a lasagna over to my house when I had to have surgery following a miscarriage." There's no doubt in her mind. She said, "That's what Catholic military women do for each other—we show up when it matters."

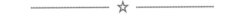

"Soul Sisters" Next Door and Overseas

Lord, please help me be attentive
to my military sister in Christ,
who might be next door
or on the other side of the world.
Mother Mary,
help me to "run in haste"
to serve her needs,
whether it is an attentive ear
to listen to her woes,
a warm shoulder to cry on
when she is sad and weary,
or a meal when

Be Humble

she and her family
are in need
and her soldier is deployed.
Help me to be a true "soul sister"
to all of my sisters in Christ.
Dear Lord,
thank You for my sisters
and their great love for me. Amen.

By Dawn's Early Light

Fatima Prayers

The Blessed Mother appeared to three simple shepherd children — Lucia dos Santos and her younger cousins, Francisco and Jacinta Marto — in Fatima, Portugal, in 1917.[50] She requested that the Rosary be prayed daily to bring peace to the world. She told the three faith-filled children that their Rosary prayers could help to stop a war and also help to prevent another. World War I was raging at the time. Our Lady also asked for the Five First Saturdays Devotion, which I will explain below.

We make all kinds of excuses for not praying a daily Rosary. I recommend starting with at least one decade a day, preferably in the morning, and building upon it throughout the day. The Rosary is powerful! It can help unite your family members, save the souls of sinners, and bring peace, to name just a few amazing benefits. St. Padre Pio called it his weapon in spiritual warfare.

Here are the five prayers the children at Fatima learned from the angel in 1916 and the Blessed Mother in 1917. We should pray these powerful prayers too.

---

[50] I tell the full story in *Our Lady of Fatima: 100 Years of Stories, Prayers, and Devotions* (Servant, 2017) and my children's chapter book, *Our Lady's Message to Three Shepherd Children and the World* (Sophia Institute Press, 2017).

Be Humble

The Pardon Prayer

The Angel of Peace, who also revealed that he was the angel of Portugal, appeared to the children three times in 1916. The following prayer is the first one he taught them.

My God,
I believe,
I adore,
I hope,
and I love Thee!

I ask pardon for those
who do not believe,
do not adore,
do not hope,
and do not love Thee.

The Angel's Prayer

Once when the angel appeared, the three children saw him prostrate before the Holy Eucharist and the precious chalice that hung suspended in the air. Worshipping the Eucharist, the angel prayed the following prayer.

Most Holy Trinity—
Father, Son, and Holy Spirit—
I adore Thee profoundly.
I offer Thee
the most precious
Body, Blood, Soul, and Divinity
of Jesus Christ, present in

By Dawn's Early Light

all the tabernacles of the world,
in reparation for the outrages,
sacrileges, and indifferences
whereby He is offended.
And through the infinite merits
of His Most Sacred Heart
and the Immaculate Heart of Mary,
I beg of Thee the conversion of poor sinners.

The Eucharistic Prayer

*During the first apparition of Our Lady of Fatima, on
May 13, 1917, the shepherd children were "moved by
an interior impulse," as Lucia later explained in her
memoirs, to say the following prayer together,*

Most Holy Trinity,
I adore Thee!
My God, my God,
I love Thee in the
Most Blessed Sacrament.

Be Humble

The Sacrifice Prayer

The Blessed Mother taught the shepherd children to offer all their personal sacrifices to God and to pray this prayer. It is a prayer that we can say often as well:

O my Jesus,
I offer this for love of Thee,
for the conversion of sinners,
and in reparation for the sins committed
against the Immaculate Heart of Mary.

The Rosary Decade Prayer

The Blessed Mother stressed the critical importance of praying the Rosary daily for the conversion of sinners and for peace in the world. She asked that the following prayer be recited at the end of each decade.

O my Jesus, forgive us our sins,
save us from the fires of Hell,
lead all souls to Heaven,
especially those in most need
of Thy mercy.

These are prayers that we can try to commit to memory and pray often. Particularly we want to pray the Decade Prayer each day with our Rosary. The Sacrifice Prayer can be easily voiced quietly in our hearts each time we offer up an inconvenience, pain, or suffering. We can even pray it throughout our daily routine, offering everything up for Heaven's plans.

I Am the Handmaid of the Lord

Take some time to ponder how our Lord is speaking to your heart. Do you take the time to get closer to Jesus' Mother, Mary? Jesus gave us the gift of His Mother when He was hanging on the Cross. She is our mother, and she has much to teach us. St. John Paul II reminds us, "This woman of faith, Mary of Nazareth, the mother of God, has been given to us as a model in our pilgrimage of faith."[51] Let us turn to Mother Mary, asking her help in growing closer to Jesus and in becoming the beautiful Catholic women we are called to be.

Prayer to Mother Mary

Teach me to be virtuous
like you, Mother Mary.
Protect me and guide me.
Mary, Mother of Jesus,
be mother to me now. Amen.

[51] St. John Paul II, Homily, October 6, 1979, Washington, D.C.

6

Be of Service

*Amen, I say to you, whatever you did for one of
these least brothers of mine, you did for me.*

—Matthew 25:40, NABRE

Jesus said that whatever we do to the least of our brothers, we do to Him. How, then, can we fight a war? T. S. Eliot said, "War is not a life: it is a situation, one which may neither be ignored or accepted."[52] Countless people grapple with the meaning of war—specifically because Jesus told us, "Blessed are the peacemakers" (Matt. 5:9). The Fifth Commandment forbids the intentional destruction of human life. The *Catechism* tells us, "Because of the evils and injustices that accompany all war, the Church insistently urges everyone to prayer and to action so that divine Goodness may free us from the ancient bondage of war"[53] (CCC 2307). So how can a Christian or a Catholic engage in war in good conscience?

Certainly, we should avoid war whenever possible. St. Augustine wrote, "War should be waged only as a necessity ... that peace may be obtained." St. Thomas Aquinas said that just war has "the object of securing peace, of repressing evil, and supporting the good." He gave three conditions for a just war:

1. It must be declared and waged by lawful authority.

2. It must be truly necessary for achieving a just cause.

3. It must be conducted with the intention of restoring justice and peace.

[52] T. S. Eliot, "A Note on War Poetry."
[53] Cf. GS 81 § 4.

The *Catechism* teaches:

> Those who are sworn to serve their country in the armed forces are servants of the security and freedom of nations. If they carry out their duty honorably, they truly contribute to the common good of the nation and to the maintenance of peace.[54] (2310)

Pope Francis, in a 2016 conference in Rome on "Nonviolence and Just Peace," endorsed "active nonviolence" as the ideal alternative to armed combat. He noted, however, that although the Second Vatican Council condemned war, it supported a government's right to an armed defense under just-war principles. Deacon James Toner, a former Army officer and a military ethicist, stated, "Sometimes the only ethical avenue to take in the face of aggression is to stop it—and take military means if necessary.... There are times when we are morally justified—and morally obligated—to prevent or to stop evil."[55]

The *Catechism* elaborates on the traditional elements of just-war doctrine: "The strict conditions for legitimate defense by military force require rigorous consideration. The gravity of such a decision makes it subject to rigorous conditions of moral legitimacy." At one and the same time:

- The damage inflicted by the aggressor on the nation or community of nations must be lasting, grave, and certain;

- All other means of putting an end to it must have been shown to be impractical or ineffective;

[54] Cf. GS 79 § 5.
[55] Quoted in Gerald Korson, "When Breaking Evil Warrants War," *Legatus*, August 1, 2017, http://legatus.org/when-breaking-evil-warrants-war/.

• There must be serious prospects of success;

• The use of arms must not produce evils and disorders graver than the evil to be eliminated. The power of modern means of destruction weighs very heavily in evaluating this condition. (2309)

You Did It to Me

St. Teresa of Calcutta said, "Love is not words. It is action. Our vocation is to love." And that is exactly what she did—she loved the world and taught us all about sacrificial love. On September 10, 1946, Mother Teresa (then Sister Teresa) received what she referred to as a "call within a call" during her vocation as a religious nun. She was initially a religious sister of Our Lady of Loreto, first in Ireland and then in Calcutta. But on a train journey to her yearly retreat in Darjeeling, she distinctly heard Jesus Christ telling her that her life would be redirected in a wholly and profound new way. Our Lord called to her, "Come, be my light." This was the call to found the religious order of the Missionaries of Charity. Bit by bit, Jesus enlightened Sister Teresa about His plan.

After much study by the Church, the Missionaries of Charity religious order began and Mother Teresa donned her new habit on August 17, 1948. Throughout each day, the Missionaries of Charity connect with Jesus in two profound physical ways: first, under the appearances of consecrated bread and wine, and second, under the appearance of the broken and devastated bodies of the poorest of the poor. Mother Teresa was convinced that in order to take care of the poor and the needy, the members of her order had to nourish themselves with the Bread of Life, the

Eucharist. In speaking of the poor they connect with and whom they meet in a variety of circumstances, or "disguises," as Mother Teresa would say—the addict, the prostitute, the street beggar, the alcoholic, the lonely—she said, "If we reject them, if we do not go out to meet them, we reject Jesus Himself."

St. Teresa of Calcutta was strengthened by and lived by the words of Jesus in Matthew's Gospel. "Come, you who are blessed by my Father, inherit the kingdom prepared for you from the foundation of the world; for I was hungry and you gave me food, I was thirsty and you gave me something to drink, I was a stranger and you welcomed me, I was naked and you gave me clothing, I was sick and you took care of me, I was in prison and you visited me" (Matt. 25:34–36).

St. Teresa of Calcutta's holy life of loving service deeply touches our hearts. Do we welcome Jesus in the stranger? Do we welcome Him in our family members? He instructs us, "Just as you did it to one of the least of these who are members of the family, you did it to me" (Matt. 25:40). What do we do and not do to him? We must ponder that in our hearts.

"You Did It to Me" Prayer

Dear Lord Jesus, You teach us to reach out to others with love and to treat them as if they were You.

Most times I seem blind to the fact that You are there in my family member, my neighbor, those who are needy, and even my enemy, whom I should pray for. Sometimes I am too caught up with all my devices to notice the needs presented right in front of me.

Please open my heart to Your love. Help me to give with a generous heart, especially of my time to listen to one who needs to vent. Remind me to smile and spread Your love to all I meet, knowing that even though someone might look all put together, he may be crying in pain inside and that my smile and allowing Your love to shine through my eyes can transform his heart and soul and give him great hope. Amen.

By Dawn's Early Light

Military *Esprit De Corps*

Army wife Elizabeth Tomlin shared with me about her involvement in the military. She said that she and her husband, Greg, grew up as "military brats." She explained, "My Dad is a retired Marine, and my father-in-law retired from the Army." Greg has served in the military for sixteen years thus far. Elizabeth noted, "Empirically, military parents beget military children. Much like the Catholic Faith, there is an esprit de corps that military parents impart to their children. The patriotic desire to serve our nation and the value of the military are familiar and held in high esteem in military families."

Elizabeth said she feels "that military life has to be vocational. If a person feels called to volunteer to defend the freedoms of our country, then he or she should join the military." She has served as president of the MCCW and has served in the CWOC. She spends a lot of time volunteering at her children's schools, as well sitting on football and swimming-pool bleachers to cheer her children on.

The saints inspire Elizabeth, as do good spiritual reading and media. For fun and relaxation, Elizabeth likes to dig in the dirt. She, like me, loves gardening. She said, "I do great thinking while gardening. Somehow there is satisfaction in watching little cucumber sprouts grow into unruly vines that produce veggies until the first frost." She missed her gardening when her husband was stationed in El Paso at Fort Bliss.

Like so many other military personnel and their families, Elizabeth knows that change is a continual way of life. "Military life requires us to be adaptive to new surroundings," Elizabeth pointed out. "We are resourceful and scrappy because of this. Seeing my kids adapt to new surroundings gives me pride and inspires me."

Be of Service

We Need to Serve Jesus in Others

We might ask ourselves a couple of questions: Are we attentive to those who need our help? How about our next-door neighbors? Jesus instructed us to serve our brothers and sisters, especially those who need our help. Further, He explained that when we do so, we actually serve Him! And He said that we will be judged by how we love our brothers and sisters — the "least" of them! Just read Matthew 25:31–46. St. Teresa of Calcutta lived her entire ministry based on Jesus' words in that passage.

For the most part, military personnel and their families are amazingly helpful to one another. They serve our country and one another, and are very quick to do so, and they're welcoming. But, there are "off days." Perhaps someone was not attentive when he or she could have been a great help. Our being observant and attentive to those around us can make all the difference in the world to someone who needs our help. We can certainly pray for the grace to be more generous with our time and our love.

Elizabeth Tomlin told me a story that I will share with you now with her permission. She was a single mom for a time who raised her first two babies alone. She said, "I became a single mom when my son was four and my daughter was five weeks old." She told me, "I knew how to raise babies alone." Elizabeth eventually remarried. "After my husband and I married and had our youngest child, my husband was deployed for a year." This was not what Elizabeth had expected. "I was furious! This was supposed to be the baby I did not have to raise alone." But she had no choice. "There I was, living in New York, working a full-time job, and raising three kids alone." She was exhausted.

"I distinctly recall one day, there had been a blizzard," Elizabeth shared. "I went outside to shovel the snow while a movie was playing inside for the kids." Snow falls deep and piles up fast in some winters in New York. "There was so much snow piled on either side of the driveway that the piles were taller than me." Elizabeth knew she had to do her best to clear the driveway. Despite her determined efforts, she said, "I could not hurl the snow any higher." She continued, "The service member who lived across the street emerged from his house during my shoveling. He wheeled a snow blower out of his garage, and, in about ten minutes, he removed the snow from his driveway." Elizabeth was hoping against all hope that he would take notice of her struggling to clear hers. Sometimes it is difficult to ask for help. Elizabeth said, "I hoped that he would take pity on me and help me move the snow, since he knew that my husband was deployed." But, sadly, that was not the case. "To my disappointment, as soon as he finished the last inch of his driveway, he wheeled the snow blower back into his house and shut the garage." Her heart immediately sank. But she kept at that monster of a chore.

"After about an hour, I finally finished the shoveling." Now, she would be able to get out with the kids. "I went inside, and dressed the kids to make a trek to the grocery store. After loading the kids into my car, which was parked in the garage," Elizabeth observed the unthinkable. "I discovered that the wind had blown a four-foot snowdrift against my garage. I would have to re-shovel in order to leave my house."

That was it—the last straw for Elizabeth. "At this point, I pretty much lost it," she explained. "I remember taking the snow shovel, hurling it into my front yard, bursting into tears, and unloading my babies into the house." In that moment, she says, "I felt completely defeated." Elizabeth also felt completely alone and unable to do something as simple as get to the store to get provisions for her family. "I was completely heartbroken and exhausted. I was alone, six months into the deployment, trying to get to the grocery store, and felt like I could not accomplish anything." She reflected on that trying moment and said, "In hindsight, it was really not the end of the world, but in the moment, I felt very, very weak."

Serving Spiritual Needs

Military chaplains are pillars for military spiritual life. I am told that there is a need for more chaplains. Elizabeth Tomlin talked to me about the importance of pastoral presence and how that unique presence gave her husband strength at a harrowing moment. She said, "My husband was on a field exercise and very tragically, a soldier was killed during the training." It was almost impossible to fathom. Elizabeth explained, "My husband says that during the chaos of the situation, he looked to his side and saw the Catholic chaplain standing next to him." In that moment, "the chaplain's presence was the grounding reassurance to press on." Elizabeth reiterated, "The pastoral presence is so important."

"What is even more important," she added, "is having the sacraments available to service members." At times, it is even more critical. "If submarine or ship deploys without a Catholic priest, sailors cannot have access to the Eucharist or the other sacraments," Elizabeth pointed out. "We have to pray for vocations for this reason."

We can do that. Let's pray for those vocations.

By Dawn's Early Light

Prayer of a Chaplain

My God, I am unworthy,
but You have chosen me to serve with Your love.
Many times I feel ill-equipped.
Please bless me with every grace I need
to care for the spiritual needs of those
You have placed in my care.

Grant me strength, courage,
and a tremendous amount of love
to pour out to others.

As I counsel and bless Your soldiers,
please be there in our midst.

Mother Mary, protect us please.
Jesus, I trust in You! Amen.

Prayer to Jesus and Mary

Dear Jesus and Blessed Mother Mary,
please watch over me and my family
as we strive to serve all with Christ's love.
Please grant us every grace. Amen.

God calls us to continual loving service to others. We need to
pray for the graces to do so each and every day. Jesus says, "Truly
I tell you, just as you did it to one of the least of these who are
members of the family, you did it to me." May we always listen and
look attentively to the needs around us and love with Christ's love.

7

Be Selfless, Forgiving, and Merciful

Live by the spirit, I say, and do not gratify the desires of the
flesh. For what the flesh desires is opposed to the spirit, and what
the spirit desires is opposed to the flesh; for these are opposed
to each other, to prevent you from doing what you want.

—Galatians 5:16–17

Every day we battle the world, the flesh, and the devil in some way. Every day a battle for souls rages on. For the most part, it is an invisible battle and we might not take notice. But we absolutely need to be aware that the devil, who does not sleep, wants to snatch as many souls as he can for the terrors of Hell. The reality of Hell and evil might seem scary, but the Blessed Mother didn't hesitate to show the reality of Hell to the three precious shepherd children at Fatima. The terrifying vision lasted only a moment, but the children never forgot it. The young visionaries dedicated the remainder of their lives to saving souls from Hell by offering many Rosaries and many penances and sacrifices. We are called to do the same.

Don't Be a Frog

Are you doing battle with the things of the world? I hope so. Each day we are to put on the armor of Christ and pick up our weapon—our rosary beads—and put one foot in front of the other to pray and walk in faith. Servant of God Fulton Sheen used the analogy of a frog in hot water to illustrate the importance of not getting comfortable with the world and its deceptions, which will drag us down to Hell. He told the story this way:

> Take a frog. Put that frog in water. Then heat the water imperceptibly, day by day, increasing the temperature

until the water is boiling. At no point during the increase of temperature will the frog ever offer resistance. It will never realize that the water is too hot—until it's dead. That's the way we are spiritually. We just become used to the temperature of the world. And we don't realize that it is gradually possessing us, until we are in its grip. So we are doing battle therefore with triteness, shallowness, and dullness, and we have to resist and begin to go in the other direction.[56]

His words are wise indeed. We must not become complacent. Otherwise, we are cooperating with our own spiritual death. Remember, our Lord said that He does not tolerate a lukewarm soul (Rev. 3:16). We must be alive in our faith!

War must be, while we defend our lives against a destroyer who would devour all; but I do not love the bright sword for its sharpness, nor the arrow for its swiftness, nor the warrior for his glory. I love only that which they defend.[57]

The Dignity of Women

Do we know our worth? Many times we women are so worn down by life's struggles and the variety of ugly stuff that daily bombards us from the world that we might forget about our beautiful dignity in God's eyes. At times, we might also be too exhausted even to care about our dignity. We could be in survival mode, trying to get ourselves in or out of some dark foxhole or feeling as if it's another "groundhog day." That's why it's so important

[56] Sheen and Dieterich, *Through the Year with Fulton Sheen*, 34.
[57] Said by Faramir in J. R. R. Tolkien, *The Two Towers*, bk. 4, chap. 5.

to surround ourselves, as best as we can, with like-minded and faith-filled women who will bolster our faith, remind us of our dignity, and help us to keep on the straight and narrow. God wants us to know about our dignity, to acknowledge it even. And, further, to use it to be a brilliant light to others! So many are struggling with heavy crosses and wounded hearts. We can be a healing balm of love to them. We are all in this together, right? Let's snap out of our complacency or our doubt about our exquisite God-given dignity so that we can help to change the world—yes, that's right—even one woman at a time! God is counting on us.

St. John Paul II wrote extensively on the dignity and vocation of woman in his Apostolic Letter *Mulieris Dignitatem*. He also wrote a *Letter to Women*, in which he thanked every woman "for the simple fact of being a woman!" He said, "Through the insight which is so much a part of your womanhood, you enrich the world's understanding and help to make human relations more honest and authentic."[58] He ended his beautiful reflection with a prayer: "May Mary, Queen of Love, watch over women and their mission in service of humanity, of peace, of the spread of God's Kingdom!"[59] Beautiful! I highly recommend that you read these two documents, which I guarantee will edify and strengthen you. You might want to consider studying them in a group setting, maybe with a group of your Catholic girlfriends.

I consider St. John Paul II to be a hero to women. He really understood our hearts. He had a great love for the Blessed Mother and was so taken by St. Louis de Montfort's teachings on Mary, that, as Karol Wojtyla, he adopted St. Louis's phrase

[58] John Paul II, *Letter to Women* (June 29, 1995), no. 2.
[59] Ibid., no. 12.

Totus tuus ("Totally yours") as his motto as a bishop and later as pope.[60]

In *Mulieris Dignitatem* St. John Paul II wrote:

A woman's dignity is closely connected with the love which she receives by the very reason of her femininity; it is likewise connected with the love which she gives in return.... The moral and spiritual strength of a woman is joined to her awareness that God entrusts the human being to her in a special way. Of course, God entrusts every human being to each and every other human being. But this entrusting concerns women in a special way — precisely by reason of their femininity — and this in a particular way determines their vocation. The moral force of women, which draws strength from this awareness and this entrusting, expresses itself in a great number of figures of the Old Testament, of the time of Christ, and of later ages right up to our own day. A woman is strong because of her awareness of this entrusting, strong because of the fact that God "entrusts the human being to her," always and in every way, even in the situations of social discrimination in which she may find herself. This awareness and this fundamental vocation speaks to women of the dignity which they receive from God himself, and this makes them "strong" and strengthens their vocation.[61]

---

[60] St. Louis de Montfort (1673–1716) said to Mary, "I am totally yours, and all that I have is yours."

[61] John Paul II, Apostolic Letter *Mulieris Dignitatem: On the Dignity and Vocation of Women* (August 15, 1988), no. 30.

We Are Entrusted with the Human Being!

Did you catch a couple of the most important words in the preceding passage from St. John Paul II? I don't mean just "dignity," which is extremely important, of course. But I am getting at "entrusting" and "awareness" and the fact that a "woman is strong"! Remember, St. John Paul II said that the moral force of women draws strength from this awareness and this entrusting. How could we be strong and confident in our feminine gifts if we are not even aware of them—aware that God Himself gives us these special gifts? Not only that: we are entrusted with the *human being*! Wow! That should open our eyes and our hearts!

Everyone needs a mother. Ultimately, the Virgin Mary is a mother to us all. But many don't know her. We women fill such an important role as spiritual mothers to those around us, even if we are not biological or adoptive mothers—and not just our own family members. Edith Stein (1891–1942) wrote, "Everywhere the need exists for maternal sympathy and help, and thus we are able to recapitulate in one word 'motherliness' that which we have developed as the characteristic value of woman."[62] She goes on to stress that our spiritual motherhood to others must not stop in our own families. Specifically, she says, "The motherliness must be that which does not remain within the narrow circle of blood relations or of personal friends; but in accordance with the model of the Mother of Mercy, it must have its root in universal divine love for all who are there, belabored and burdened."[63]

I love how Edith Stein described a woman's love for another coming forth and bearing fruit within her actions and care—even

---

[62] Joanne Mosley, *Edith Stein: Woman of Prayer* (Leominster, UK: Gracewing, 2004), 85.
[63] Ibid., 258.

in the simple case of a sore foot. It's what I call, "the mom in me" operating. She wrote:

> Everywhere she meets with a human being, she will find opportunity to sustain, to counsel, to help. If the factory worker or the office employee would only pay attention to the spirits of the persons who work with her in the same room, she would prevail upon trouble-laden hearts to be opened to her through a friendly word, a sympathetic question; she will find out where the shoe is pinching and will be able to provide relief.[64]

Are we seeking to bring relief to those whom God puts in our midst? Even a simple smile can help to transform someone's day. I wholeheartedly believe this. It is something profound that I learned from my dear spiritual mother, Mother Teresa, who was famous for saying, "Do small things with great love."

In *Life Is Worth Living*, Servant of God Archbishop Fulton Sheen wrote, "The man is the guardian of nature, but the woman is the custodian of life. Therefore, in whatever she does, she must have some occasion to be kind and merciful to others."[65] We have to believe that God has entrusted women with the care of the human being and with amazing feminine gifts that are meant to be shared and even to heal others—our families and beyond! But, before that can happen, we need to allow God to heal our own hearts and souls.

[64] "Woman's Value in National Life" in Edith Stein, *Essays on Woman*, Collected Works of Edith Stein (Washington, D.C.: ICS Publications, 1987), 264.

[65] "Women Who Do Not Fail" in Fulton J. Sheen, *Life Is Worth Living* (San Francisco: Ignatius Press, 1999).

Be Selfless, Forgiving, and Merciful

Let's go to the foot of the Cross in our prayers and soak in Jesus' amazing love for us. Let's pray and ponder there at Jesus' feet at the tabernacle whenever we are able to go for a respite. It might not be for an hour, but maybe for just fifteen minutes, as time allows. Many times, our prayers at Jesus' feet will be just a moment here and there, lifting up our hearts while trudging through our days, trying to take care of all of the things we do in caring for our families, as well as praying for those under our "command" or to whom we "report" for duty. But while we are with Jesus after we have received the Bread of Life in Holy Communion or at the foot of the Cross in meditation or while in front of the Blessed Sacrament, let's be sure to thank Him for the gift of caring for the human being and for all of the gifts He bestows upon us to do so.

Let's look at a reflection on women's dignity from a cardinal who pondered and prayed in prison during dark days and nights in solitary confinement. In his beautiful prison reflection "The Dignity of Women," Cardinal Nguyen Van Thuan wrote about the contrast between society's view of women and Jesus' attitude toward women and their magnificent dignity. As well, he directed our thoughts to Mary, the mother of God:

> When considering the call of women, some people think only of the vocation of motherhood. From antiquity, Oriental societies identified woman with a fertile womb; even modern Western societies often consider woman only in relation to her sensuality.
>
> Jesus considered and treated women as human beings. And it is in the sublime setting of our humanity that the dignity and true happiness of men and women is realized. Very often, as is seen throughout Scripture and history, it

is because of women that men are able to listen to God and to live the mystery of grace with its demands.[66]

Mary, Mother of God

Mary, mother of God,
you are the model of faith
for all of us—men and women.

You are representative of all humanity,
because you welcomed
the most sublime of all graces:
the presence of God on earth.

God's presence transforms all things,
even if no exterior change is apparent.
The most marvelous mystery
in the history of humanity
was accomplished through your
offering and collaboration:
"God became man."

For having believed,
you are blessed and worthy of praise.

Your existence is the fountain
of joy and blessing
for all women and men
who believe as you believed. Amen.

[66] Nguyễn, *Prayers of Hope*, 92–93.

Be Selfless, Forgiving, and Merciful

Are We Raising the Bar?

Servant of God Archbishop Sheen reflected on the dignity and gifts of women. I absolutely love that he pointed out how a woman's dignity affects men and even the whole of civilization. He wrote, "The level of any civilization is always the level of its womanhood.... Since a woman is loved, it follows that the nobler a woman is, the nobler man will have to be deserving of that love. That love is why the level of any civilization is always the level of its womanhood."[67] We might ponder what we women are actively doing to raise the level of our civilization. Are we living noble and virtuous lives?

Confession, Conversion, and Forgiveness

We read something profound in Luke's Gospel: "I shall get up and go to my father and I shall say to him, 'Father, I have sinned against heaven and against you'" (Luke 15:18). The story of the prodigal son touches us all. Each one of us has in some way chosen foolishly, casting away the home that God has provided for us in Heaven because we fell for the seductions and the allurements of the darkened world. The sacrament of Confession is the answer to peace of heart and will bring us to the state of grace once again, as well as strengthen us for our journey. Our Father in Heaven welcomes us with open arms.

In addition to seeking forgiveness, we need to forgive those who have harmed us. That might be difficult, but God will grant us the graces to desire to do so. Our hearts will be at peace once we have forgiven. We must remember that Our

---

[67] Sheen, "Women Who Do Not Fail."

195

Lord will forgive us our sins to the extent that we are willing to forgive others. "Forgive us our sins, as we forgive those who trespass against us."

Act of Contrition

Many Catholics pray the Act of Contrition regularly, particularly during the sacrament of Confession and before going to bed during a prayerful review of the day (or examination of conscience).

O my God,
I am heartily sorry for
having offended Thee,
and I detest all my sins,
because I dread the loss of Heaven,
and the pains of Hell;
but most of all because
they offend Thee, my God,
who are all good and
deserving of all my love.
I firmly resolve,
with the help of Thy grace,
to confess my sins,
to do penance,
and to amend my life. Amen.

Be Selfless, Forgiving, and Merciful

The *Catechism* teaches about conversion of heart and confessing our sins:

> Jesus' call to conversion and penance, like that of the prophets before him, does not aim first at outward works, "sackcloth and ashes," fasting and mortification, but at *conversion of heart, interior conversion*. Without this, penances remain sterile and false; however, interior conversion urges expression in visible signs, gestures, and works of penance (cf. Joel 2:12–13; Isa. 1:16–17; Matt. 6:1–6, 16–18).
>
> Interior repentance is a radical reorientation of our whole life, a return, a conversion to God with all our heart, an end of sin, a turning away from evil, with repugnance toward the evil actions we have committed. At the same time it entails the desire and resolution to change one's life, with hope in God's mercy and trust in the help of his grace." (1430–1431)

Prayer for One's Vocation in Life

Lord, make me a better person:
more considerate toward others,
more honest with myself,
more faithful to you.

Help me to find my true vocation in life
and grant that through it
I may find happiness myself
and bring happiness to others.

By Dawn's Early Light

Grant, Lord, that those whom you call
to enter priesthood or religious life
may have the generosity to answer your call,
so that those who need your help
may always find it.

We ask this through Christ our Lord. Amen.[68]

Philippians 2:5-8

Let the same mind be in you that was in Christ Jesus,
who, though he was in the form of God,
  did not regard equality with God
  as something to be exploited,
but emptied himself,
  taking the form of a slave,
  being born in human likeness.
And being found in human form,
  he humbled himself
  and became obedient to the point of death —
  even death on a cross.

---

[68] Jacquelyn Lindsey, *Prayer Book for Catholics* (Huntington, IN: Our Sunday Visitor, 2005).

Be Selfless, Forgiving, and Merciful

Prayer for Guidance
St. Basil the Great (329–379)

O Lord our God, we beseech You,
to give us the gift we need.
Steer the ship of our life to Yourself,
the quiet harbor of all storm-stressed souls.

Show us the course which we are to take.
Renew in us the spirit of docility.
Let your Spirit curb our fickleness;
guide and strengthen us to perform
what is for our own good,
to keep Your commandments
and ever to rejoice in Your glorious
and vivifying presence.

Yours is the glory and praise
for all eternity. Amen.

I Am the Handmaid of the Lord

At the beginning of this chapter, we read the words "Live by the Spirit." We also discussed our magnificent dignity as women, possessing many gifts with which we are to serve and even "mother" others. We were also reminded about our great mission in caring for the human being! We went over the need to convert our hearts, to forgive, and to be forgiven. Take a few moments now to ponder these things in your heart.

Prayer to Jesus

Dear Jesus,
help me to be
the woman you call me to be.

Help me to reach out
with my mother's heart
to serve those you put in my midst.

Day by day,
please enlighten me
to the depths of my mission
in the sublimity of caring for others. Amen.

8

Be Loyal

---- ☆ ----

*No one has greater love than this, to lay
down one's life for one's friends.*

—John 15:13

In wartime we must worry less whether God is on our side and worry more about whether we are on God's side," stated Servant of God Fulton Sheen.[69] We must "fight the good fight of the faith" (1 Tim. 6:12) and always put on the armor of God, even simply for survival in the spiritual life. As Scripture tells us:

> Put on the whole armor of God, so that you may be able to stand against the wiles of the devil. For our struggle is not against enemies of blood and flesh, but against the rulers, against the authorities, against the cosmic powers of this present darkness, against the spiritual forces of evil in the heavenly places. Therefore, take up the whole armor of God, so that you may be able to withstand on that evil day, and having done everything, to stand firm. (Eph. 6:11–13)

Does the notion of being in a spiritual battle and about the need for putting on the whole armor of God sound a bit doom and gloom? It might be disconcerting, but it is necessary to understand that the battle for souls is a reality, and we must acknowledge it. As I mentioned in the previous chapter, there is an invisible, yet critical battle being waged every single day. If we are not careful, we can lose our souls. We have been placed in this world to work out our salvation on this pilgrimage through

---

[69] *Fulton Sheen's Wartime Prayer Book*, 9.

life. We are also called to be a brilliant light of faith to others so that we can help them get to Heaven as well.

What do we need to do? Again, Scripture tells us:

> Stand therefore, and fasten the belt of truth around your waist, and put on the breastplate of righteousness. As shoes for your feet put on whatever will make you ready to proclaim the gospel of peace. With all of these, take the shield of faith, with which you will be able to quench all the flaming arrows of the evil one. Take the helmet of salvation, and the sword of the Spirit, which is the word of God. (Eph. 6:14–17)

Walking in Faith, Giving Hope to Others

St. Teresa of Calcutta chose simple sandals to walk in faith in the hot climate of Calcutta, India, where she proclaimed the "gospel of peace" to each person whom God put in her path — those from whom she pulled maggots after picking them up out of the gutters, each leper she cared for, and every baby and child abandoned by leper parents whom she placed in loving adoptive homes.

One time, some people outside of Mother Teresa's Nirmal Hriday (Immaculate Heart of Mary) home for the dying in Calcutta were in an uproar. They wanted Mother out! Even though the majority of the people recognized that she was providing an invaluable service and relieving the city of the embarrassment of people dying in the street, some people complained that she was trying to convert people to Christianity. A thorough inspection was made with the intention of closing down her work. It was found, however, that the sisters fed, medicated, and cleansed emaciated sick and dying people. The investigators reported back to the complainers and said that they would close down Mother Teresa's shelters if the complainers got their own mothers and sisters to do the same work. The opposition immediately stopped! No one was willing to do the same loving work. Mother Teresa strove to do what our Lord called her to do. In a sense, Mother Teresa laid down her life for others. What is our Lord calling us to do in our own "Calcutta"?

Recalling the verse above from Ephesians, St. Pio of Pietrelcina (1887–1968), beloved by many and known for bearing the Stigmata (the five wounds of Christ), used his rosary as a "weapon" and "a shield of faith" to "quench all the flaming arrows of the evil one." Do we keep our rosary with us and pray with it? Do we believe in the power of prayer?

Like Mother Teresa, Padre Pio saw Jesus in the sick and suffering. He was instrumental in building a hospital on nearby Mount Gargano. As his spiritual influence grew, the voices of detractors did as well. Complaints were filed with the Holy Office, and eventually Padre Pio was ordered not to answer correspondence and to discontinue hearing confessions, and even his Masses were curtailed. Out of obedience, Padre Pio submitted to all these restrictions, but his ministry continued to grow. There were plans to move him to another location, but due to fear of a mass uproar, he was allowed to remain at San Giovanni Rotundo.

God gave St. Pio many gifts to serve people and used him to give people hope as they began to rebuild their lives after World War I. Padre Pio and his spiritual gifts of the stigmata, perfume, and bilocation were sure signs of God working in their midst, and they led the weary people back to their faith. Padre Pio, in essence, laid down his life for the faithful he served and was obedient to his superiors and trusted God's holy will in his life. Do we lay down our lives and trust God?

By Dawn's Early Light

I Am More Valuable Than Sparrows

"Are not two sparrows sold for a penny? Yet no one of them will fall to the ground apart from your Father. And even the hairs on your head are counted. So do not be afraid; you are more value than the sparrows" (Matt. 10:29–31). Jesus encouraged His disciples by giving the example of the sparrows and the hairs on their heads. Right before the word about the sparrows, He told them, "Do not fear those who kill the body but cannot kill the soul"; rather, He said they should "fear him who can destroy both soul and body in hell" (Matt. 10:28).

There is no getting out of Hell! We must work out our salvation while on earth within the details of our daily lives. We must not allow ourselves to get swept up into the wiles and wickedness of the devil, who tries to persuade us to take our eyes off Heaven and its rewards by getting us infatuated with the pleasures and false promises of the world. Yes, God knows everything—He knows when a simple bird such as a sparrow (which was worth only half a penny) falls to the ground, and He knows how many hairs we have on our heads. We can wholeheartedly trust Him with our lives. He wants us with Him in Heaven forever and not in the eternal damnation of Hell.

Be Loyal

St. Teresa of Avila's Prayer

Let nothing disturb you.
Let nothing frighten you.
All things are passing away.
God never changes.
Patience obtains all things.
Whoever has God lacks nothing;
God alone suffices.

Love bears all things,
believes all things,
endures all things.

—1 Corinthians 13:7

By Dawn's Early Light

In Harm's Way

Perhaps the scariest part of military life is being in harm's way. For both military personnel and their families, the uncertainty and the risk of harm or even death can be utterly terrifying. It's a fear that most cannot fully comprehend but can perhaps imagine to a certain extent. Because of living with such terrors, many faithful military people cling tightly to their faith. Staying connected with other faith-filled Christians aids immensely.

I met a man named Tom, who told me about a time when he was serving as an Army sergeant in Vietnam and God profoundly touched his heart at a harrowing time. He said, "I always carried a rosary in my pocket." Tom developed a devotion to the Blessed Mother as a young boy. His father made sure that his son always had a rosary even as an adult. In Vietnam Tom carried a plastic rosary.

"One night, I had given up hope of coming home alive and got into an argument with some of the guys in my platoon." Tom was frustrated with his fellow soldiers. He explained, "When we went on patrol, we had to seek out the enemy. Many, but not all, men were very harsh and disrespectful to the women and children." Tom did not want to be like them. "I personally wouldn't do that. I won them over by caring for them, like giving them food or whatever I had." Tom explained, "They were more open, and most of the time they were honest with me." He added, "The other guys didn't trust them, so they abused the women and children to find out about the enemy." He reiterated, "They wanted me to be like them, and I wouldn't."

So, on that fateful day in Vietnam, Tom was very stressed and was feeling a deep loss of hope. He told me, "I locked and loaded my rifle and told them to lay off, and I began getting hostile, when at that moment my company commander came up to me and said, 'Put the gun down,' and I did."

Tom needed a huge dose of hope in that moment. He recalled, "My uncle who was an alcoholic had sent me a Bible, which was lying next to my cot." He continued to recount the intense moment: "I don't know why, but I took the Bible and opened it and laid it across my chest and, at that moment, felt peace that was so beautiful and calming." Right then, Tom had no doubt about the outcome. He said, "I knew then that the Lord would carry me through this difficult time." Tom said he is certain that he was able to return home from the war "due to our Blessed Mother and her Son."

There are many frightening aspects of military life. Army wife Elizabeth Tomlin explained some of the impact that it has on families. Especially during deployments or training exercises, military families recognize that their service member's profession is inherently dangerous. Elizabeth shared her own fears: "When my husband has served in units that have lost soldiers, it is worrisome to watch him go back into harm's way." Then again, her husband reminds her that "if you are worrying, you are not praying hard enough." It's certainly difficult not to worry or be concerned for what might happen. We must trust in God, however, staying in the state of grace through the sacraments of the Church, and a commitment to prayer is not only essential for spiritual survival, but can alleviate some of the stress and strain.

Psalm 91:11

For he will command his angels concerning you,
to guard you in all your ways.

I Am the Handmaid of the Lord

We need to be mindful of St. Paul's words:

Stand therefore, and fasten the belt of truth around your waist, and put on the breastplate of righteousness. As shoes for your feet put on whatever will make you ready to proclaim the gospel of peace. With all of these, take the shield of faith, with which you will be able to quench all the flaming arrows of the evil one. Take the helmet of salvation, and the sword of the Spirit, which is the word of God.

Prayer to Jesus, Mary, and Joseph

I do not know what lies ahead.
I only have this moment right now.
Please watch over me
and grant me every grace
to take in Your love right now
and be willing to lay down my life
in the way I am called to do.

Jesus, Mary, and Joseph,
please be with me and help me. Amen.

Part 3

Prayers for Every Occasion

———————— ☆ ————————

To you, O Lord, I lift up my soul.
O my God, in you I trust;
do not let me be put to shame;
do not let my enemies exult over me.

—Psalm 25:1–2

9

Ask for Courage, Strength, and Protection

Have I not commanded you? Be strong and of good courage; be not frightened, neither be dismayed; for the Lord your God is with you wherever you go.

—Joshua 1:9

Whether on the battlefield fighting a war or on the home front juggling demands, challenges, and a myriad of crises in being associated with the military, we should recall Archbishop Sheen's words:

> I must not be ashamed if I am fearful and if my whole being shrinks in dread, for the Lord in the Garden before going to the Battle of Calvary prayed: "If it be possible, let this cup pass from me; nevertheless, not as I will, but as thou wilt" (Matt. 26:39).
>
> What I must fear is my unwillingness to fulfill the will of God as revealed by the present circumstances of life. Not my will but thine be done.[70]

It's okay to be fearful at times. But we need to pray and to recognize the amazing power of prayer to help us to overcome our fears. We can offer our fear to God. We must remember that in the Garden of Olives, before the Crucifixion, Jesus prayed that His Father's holy will, not His own, be done. We, too, need to pray for God's holy will in our lives each and every day—in easy times and tough times.

Army wife Diane Joyce Bridon said that a few things stand out in her mind that scare her about military life. She worries about her husband, and specifically, she said, about the possibility

---

[70] *Fulton Sheen's Wartime Prayer Book*, 20.

of "losing my husband in war, or that he might even be killed by an angry soldier at work, since he is now a Commander of eight hundred plus soldiers and has to, at times, administer military justice." Diane also recalled a time when her husband was away because of a deployment and she grew in her faith and discerned some important spiritual matters.

She said to me, "When my husband was deployed in Bagram, Afghanistan, we were stationed in Heidelberg, Germany. I felt called to withdraw from certain friendships that were not good for me and began to read your book *Grace Café*.[71] Each night I would read a chapter or two and then go to sleep while reflecting on it. During Lent I felt called to attend Adoration on weekdays." Diane realized that she was growing in her faith during her husband's deployment. Fears of the unknown were lifting; faith was increasing. "I saw myself growing closer to Christ, and the lonesomeness I felt earlier because of the absence of my spouse began to dissipate."

Walking on Water?

Recall that St. Peter, walking on the water, began to sink when he took his eyes off his Lord Jesus, who was calling to him. It was dark, and Peter was remembering the fierce winds and the unruly waves that had battered the terrified disciples' old fishing boat just moments earlier. At first, Jesus appeared like a ghost out on the water, but He quickly identified Himself. "Take heart, it is I; do not be afraid."

Peter answered, "Lord, if it is you, command me to come to you on the water." "Come," Jesus simply instructed. Peter got out of

---

[71] Now entitled *Catholic Wisdom for a Mother's Heart*.

the boat. He was okay for a few seconds, when he trusted Jesus, but as soon as he doubted his ability to stay afloat, down he went! Maybe through the darkness it was hard to trust. Perhaps the strength of the storm rattled his brain and caused him to fear. But the good news is that as soon as the sinking Peter, who, by the way, was an experienced fisherman cried out, "Lord, save me!" Jesus immediately rescued him, grabbing Peter's arm and lifting him safely out of the frightening waves. Jesus gently rebuked Peter: "You of little faith, why did you doubt?" They both got into the boat, and the stormy winds settled down. Everything became still, and the witnesses in the boat immediately worshipped Jesus, saying, "Truly you are the Son of God" (Matt. 14:22–33).

How often do we doubt when we take our eyes off God? How many times are we in situations when our Lord can say to us, "You of little faith, why did you doubt?" I am absolutely sure that it is an everyday occurrence in most people's lives. We doubt God's ability in seemingly insignificant circumstances, as well as in huge, overpowering ones. How will I be able to make this move? How can we survive during this deployment? Will my family make new friends at our new home? How can I go on after such a loss? The list is endless. Perhaps we can work on our trust issues. Can we endeavor to get closer to Jesus' Sacred Heart and the Immaculate Heart of Mary, where we will find peace?

By Dawn's Early Light

Prayer to the Sacred Heart of Jesus (1)
St. Margaret Mary Alacoque (1647–1690)

O Heart of Love,
I put all my trust in You.
For I fear all things
from my own weakness,
but I hope for all things
from Your goodness. Amen.

Prayer to the Sacred Heart of Jesus (2)
Blessed John Henry Cardinal Newman (1801–1890)

Most sacred, most loving heart of Jesus,
You are concealed in the Holy Eucharist,
and You beat for us still.

Now, as then, You say:
"With desire I have desired."
I worship You with all
my best love and awe,
with fervent affection,
with my most subdued,
most resolved will.

For a while You take up
Your abode within me.

Oh, make my heart beat with Your heart!
Purify it of all that is earthly,
all that is proud and sensual,
of all perversity, of all disorder.

So fill it with You,
that neither the events of the day,
nor the circumstances of the time,
may have the power to ruffle it,
but that in Your love and Your fear,
it may have peace. Amen.

Prayer to the Sacred Heart of Jesus (3)
St. Margaret Mary Alacoque

O Sacred Heart of Jesus, for whom it is impossible
not to have compassion on the afflicted,
have pity on us miserable sinners
and grant us the grace that we ask of You,
through the Sorrowful and Immaculate Heart of Mary,
Your tender Mother and ours.

Hail, holy Queen, Mother of Mercy!
our life, our sweetness, and our hope!
To thee do we cry, poor banished children of Eve;
to thee do we send up our sighs, mourning
and weeping in this valley of tears.

By Dawn's Early Light

Turn, then, most gracious Advocate,
thine eyes of mercy toward us;
and after this our exile, show unto us
the blessed fruit of thy womb, Jesus;
O clement, O loving, O sweet Virgin Mary.

St. Joseph, foster father of Jesus,
pray for us. Amen.

Efficacious Novena to the Sacred Heart of Jesus

*St. Padre Pio (1887–1968) prayed this novena
every day for those who requested his prayers.*

I

O my Jesus, You have said:
"Truly I say to you,
ask and you will receive,
seek and you will find,
knock and it will be opened to you."

Behold I knock,
I seek and ask for the grace of . . .
(*mention your request*).

Our Father . . .
Hail Mary . . .
Glory Be . . .

Sacred Heart of Jesus,
I place all my trust in You.

II
O my Jesus, You have said:
"Truly I say to you, if you
ask anything of the Father in my name,
He will give it to you."

Behold, in Your name,
I ask the Father for the grace of . . .
(*mention your request*).

Our Father . . .
Hail Mary . . .
Glory Be . . .

Sacred Heart of Jesus,
I place all my trust in You.

III
O my Jesus, You have said:
"Truly I say to you, heaven and earth will pass away
but my words will not pass away."

Encouraged by Your infallible words
I now ask for the grace of . . .
(*mention your request*).

Our Father . . .
Hail Mary . . .
Glory Be . . .

Sacred Heart of Jesus,
I place all my trust in You.

Amen.

Prayer to the Sacred Heart of Jesus and the Immaculate Heart of Mary

O Heart of Jesus, pierced for our sins
and giving us Your Mother on Calvary!

O Heart of Mary, pierced by sorrow
and sharing in the sufferings
of Your divine Son for our redemption!

O sacred union of these Two Hearts!
Praised be the God of Love,
who united them together!

May we unite our hearts and every heart
so that all hearts may live in unity
in imitation of that sacred unity
that exists in these Two Hearts.

Triumph,
O Sorrowful and Immaculate
Heart of Mary!

Reign,
O Most Sacred Heart of Jesus,
in our hearts,
in our homes and families,
in the hearts of those who
as yet do not know You,
and in all nations of the world.

Establish in the hearts of all mankind
the sovereign triumph and reign
of Your Two Hearts so that the earth

may resound from pole to pole with one cry:
Blessed forever be the Most Sacred Heart of Jesus
and the Sorrowful and Immaculate Heart of Mary!

Obtain for me a greater purity of heart
and a fervent love of the spiritual life.
May all my actions be done
for the greater glory of God
in union with the Divine Heart of Jesus
and the Immaculate Heart of Mary.

Hear and answer
our prayers and intentions ...
(*mention your request*)
according to Your most merciful will.

Amen.

By Dawn's Early Light

The Noonday Devil

An obscure and mysterious "land mine" may be concealed in your day—waiting to ambush you, perhaps right around noon-day. Have you heard of "the noonday devil"? It's actually one of the seven deadly sins (which sounds kind of scary, I know!) and is also known as *acedia* or *sloth*. Those two words conjure up notions of laziness or the avoidance of work, but acedia is not simply an avoidance of work or a kind of laziness, because someone who is a workaholic could be guilty of acedia. It's more of a procrastina-tion—a slowness in listening to God. Could you have a case of the "noonday devil"? Let's take a closer look.

Men and woman in the early Church went out to the desert to seek God in silence, solitude, prayer, and penance. They no-ticed various temptations assailing them as they pursued Jesus. They compiled a list of these temptations and called them the seven deadly sins. They are pride, wrath, envy, gluttony, greed, lust, and acedia. The desert fathers called acedia the "noonday devil" because it struck at noon. That's when they were afflicted with a bombardment of temptations alluring them to do anything other than what they were supposed to be doing—even very good things, such as taking care of the poor. Father Schmitz, director of youth and young-adult ministry for the Diocese of Duluth and chaplain of the Newman Center at the University of Minnesota–Duluth, described it this way:

> Imagine you are living in a sparse hut out in the desert. From 10 a.m. until 2 p.m. the sun seems like it is suspended in the sky, unmoving and inescapable. The freshness of morning has already passed, and the cool and calm of evening have not yet arrived. All one can do is sit in one's hut and pray (or weave baskets or whatever task to which

the hermit has been committed). The profound feeling of discontent begins beating on the door of the person's mind, arguing that they ought to get up and do something else. It doesn't matter what: sometimes it is the temptation to rejoin society and spread the Gospel or serve the poor; sometimes it was the temptation to visit another hermit for a spiritual conversation. Good things! Regardless of what the temptation is, it's the impulse to "leave one's hut" and do something else—anything else.[72]

Of course, it might not happen exactly at noon, but we must be aware of the possibility of the noonday devil skulking around and planning an attack. Working and praying faithfully and staying true to our state of life can help to cure acedia. When the noonday devil strikes, it's time to recommit ourselves to our vocation and to the task at hand, to say an immediate fervent prayer, and to enter more passionately into the present moment—no matter how boring it might seem to be.

Psalm 91

You who dwell in the shelter of the Most High,
    who abide in the shade of the Almighty,
Say to the LORD, "My refuge and fortress,
    my God in whom I trust."

---

[72] Adapted from Michael Schmitz, "Fighting the 'Noon-Day Devil' of Acedia," The Catholic Spirit, February 8, 2017, http://thecatholicspirit.com/faith/focus-on-faith/seeking-answers/fighting-noon-day-devil-acedia/.

By Dawn's Early Light

He will rescue you from the fowler's snare,
    from the destroying plague,
He will shelter you with his pinions,
    and under his wings you may take refuge;
    his faithfulness is a protecting shield.
You shall not fear the terror of the night
    nor the arrow that flies by day,
Nor the pestilence that roams in darkness,
    nor the plague that ravages at noon.
Though a thousand fall at your side,
    ten thousand at your right hand,
    near you it shall not come.
You need simply watch;
    the punishment of the wicked you will see.
Because you have the LORD for your refuge
    and have made the Most High your stronghold,
No evil shall befall you,
    no affliction come near your tent.
For he commands his angels with regard to you,
    to guard you wherever you go.
With their hands they shall support you,
    lest you strike your foot against a stone.
You can tread upon the asp and the viper,
    trample the lion and the dragon.
Because he clings to me I will deliver him;
    because he knows my name I will set him on high.
He will call upon me and I will answer;
    I will be with him in distress;
    I will deliver him and give him honor.
With length of days I will satisfy him,
    and fill him with my saving power. (RSVCE)

Trust in God's Mercy in Adversity

St. Faustina, a Polish nun who helped spread the Divine Mercy devotion in the 1930s, wrote, "Patience in adversity gives power to the soul."[73] She said that her adversaries were discouraged when they saw that, even in the worst difficulties and adversities, she did not lose her interior peace or exterior balance. Perhaps you can ponder her words to Jesus about the difficulties in facing and dealing with many troubles.

She wrote: "My Jesus, despite your graces, I see and feel all my misery. I begin my day with battle and end it with battle. As soon as I conquer one obstacle, ten more appear to take its place." Does this sound familiar to you? St. Faustina continued:

> But I am not worried, because I know that this is the time of struggle, not peace. When the burden of the battle becomes too much for me, I throw myself like a child into the arms of the heavenly Father and trust I will not perish. O my Jesus, how prone I am to evil, and this forces me to be constantly vigilant. But I do not lose heart. I trust God's grace, which abounds in the worst misery.[74]

Can we throw ourselves into the arms of our heavenly Father and trust Him wholeheartedly like St. Faustina?

[73] *Diary of Saint Maria Faustina Kowalska: Divine Mercy in My Soul*, 3rd ed. (Stockbridge, MA: Marian Press, 2005), 254.
[74] Ibid., 606.

By Dawn's Early Light

A Warrior's Breastplate

St. Patrick (fifth century)

I bind unto myself today
the power of God
to hold and lead,
His eye to watch,
His might to stay,
His ear to hearken to my need;
the wisdom of my God to teach,
His hand to guide,
His shield to ward;
the word of God to give me speech,
His heavenly host to be my guard.
Christ be with me, Christ within me,
Christ behind me, Christ before me,
Christ beside me, Christ to win me,
Christ to comfort and restore me,
Christ beneath me, Christ above me,
Christ in quiet, Christ in danger,
Christ in the hearts of all who love me,
Christ in the mouth of friend and stranger.

Our Guardian Angels

We are blessed more than we know to be assisted by countless invisible holy angels, whom God created to assist mankind.

> From its beginning until death, human life is surrounded by [the angels'] watchful care and intercession (cf. Matt. 18:10; Luke 16:22; Ps. 34:7; 91:10–13; Job 33:23–24; Zech. 1:12; Tob. 12:12). "Beside each believer stands an angel as protector and shepherd leading him to life."[75] Already here on earth the Christian life shares by faith in the blessed company of angels and men united in God. (CCC 336)

Angel on the Battlefield!

Our guardian angels are powerful! I love all the angels and have even written a book about them: *Angels for Kids* (Paraclete, 2013). I did two television shows about them with my dear friend Fr. Andrew Apostoli, C.F.R.

Fr. Andrew told me a fascinating angel story, which he also recounted on his EWTN television series, *Sunday Night Prime*. Father said that a fellow Friar told him that when he was a soldier, before he became a Friar, he got separated from his unit on the battlefield and ended up behind enemy lines. Suddenly, a man came over to him and saw that he was an American soldier who had been separated and lost. The mysterious man, who showed up out of "nowhere," said, "Follow me." The soldier obeyed. The unidentified man led the soldier safely through enemy lines and

---

[75] St. Basil, *Adv. Eunomium* III, I: PG 29,656B.

directly to the tent of his commanding officer. The grateful soldier immediately went inside to report that he was back. He turned around and the unidentified man had completely vanished. Fr. Andrew emphasized that his soldier friend "always believed that the man was his guardian angel." Fr. Andrew said that since that miraculous adventure, his friend "had always had a great devotion to his guardian angel."

Prayer to My Guardian Angel

Angel of God,
my guardian dear,
to whom God's love
commits me here,
ever this day,
be at my side,
to light and guard,
rule and guide. Amen.

Ask for Courage, Strength, and Protection

Prayer to St. Michael the Archangel

St. Michael is one of the three archangels named in Scripture. The name Michael means "Who is like God?" The profit Daniel describes St. Michael as the prince who stands guard over God's people.

St. Michael the Archangel,
defend us in battle.
Be our defense
against the wickedness
and snares of the devil.
May God rebuke him,
we humbly pray,
and do thou,
O prince of the heavenly hosts,
by the power of God,
thrust into Hell Satan,
and all the evil spirits,
who prowl about the world
seeking the ruin of souls. Amen.

By Dawn's Early Light

Prayer to St. Raphael the Archangel

St. Raphael is one of the three archangels named in Scripture. The name Raphael means "God's healer."

O God,
send the archangel Raphael
to our assistance.

May he who stands forever
praising You at Your throne
present our humble petitions
to be blessed by You.

Through Christ our Lord. Amen.

Prayer to St. Gabriel the Archangel

St. Gabriel is one of the three archangels mentioned in Scripture. The name Gabriel means "Strength of God."

O God,
who from among all Your angels
chose the archangel Gabriel to announce
the mystery of the Incarnation,
mercifully grant that we
who solemnly remember him on earth
may feel the benefits of his
patronage in Heaven,
who lives and reigns
forever and ever. Amen.

Prayer to All the Angels

All you holy angels and archangels,
thrones and dominations,
principalities and powers,
virtues of Heaven,
cherubim and seraphim,
praise the Lord forever. Amen.

Act of Faith

O my God, I firmly believe
that You are one God in three divine Persons,
Father, Son, and Holy Spirit.

I believe that Your divine Son became man
and died for our sins and that He will come
to judge the living and the dead.

I believe these and all the truths
which the Holy Catholic Church teaches
because You have revealed them
who are eternal truth and wisdom,
who can neither deceive nor be deceived.

In this faith I intend to live and die. Amen.

By Dawn's Early Light

Act of Hope

O Lord God,
I hope by Your grace
for the pardon of all my sins
and after life here
to gain eternal happiness
because You have promised it
who are infinitely powerful,
faithful, kind, and merciful.

In this hope I intend to live and die. Amen.

Act of Love

O Lord God,
I love You above all things
and I love my neighbor for Your sake
because You are the highest,
infinite and perfect good,
worthy of all my love.

In this love I intend to live and die. Amen.

To You, O Lord, I Lift Up My Soul

In this chapter, we have discussed parts of our spiritual life, some fears we might face, how we might "walk on water," watching out for the "noonday devil," the angels, the Sacred Heart of Jesus and the Immaculate Heart of Mary, and more.

Do I have recourse to the holy angels and ask for their protection and assistance? Am I mindful that God has commanded me: "Be strong and courageous. Do not be afraid; do not be discouraged"? And we also have this beautiful reminder: "The Lord your God will be with you wherever you go."

Prayer of Thanksgiving

Dear Lord,
I will never understand
the immense gift of the angels
in my life until I meet You in heaven.

For now, I thank You and praise You for them.

Help me also to grow in the virtues
of faith, hope, and love.

Thank You for Your great love for me.

I love You. Amen.

10

Ask for Help in Times of Loss

Blessed are those who mourn,
for they shall be comforted.

—Matthew 5:4

Loss is never easy. Military life has more than its fair share of good-byes. At times, it is the loss of friends who are left behind when moving to another station base or when deployed. Military bonds can seem stronger than even the meanest artillery. Modern technology greatly helps to stay in touch, but at times, it's just not the same from across the miles. That fact certainly comes into play when you wish you could ask your dear neighbor to watch your little one for just an hour while you tend to a necessary task; or when you need the shoulder of your dear sister in Christ to cry on; or when you want to celebrate a milestone happily by clinking your wine glasses together. But, alas, she's no longer right next door.

"Moving is hard for me," said Army wife Kim Miller. "Every time. And I find myself saying, at some point, 'What if I never make any friends here?'" Each time Kim questions whether she'll make new friends, her husband laughs. Kim quips, "Because it has almost become part of our moving routine — for me to panic about not making good, deep connections with people at our new assignment," Kim recalled. "As our kids get older, I find this worry about being lonely has intensified because now I worry about the kids making friends, too." Time and patience come into play. Kim added, "My husband reminds me we have to give it time; and we always find a new Army family."

Much more painful is the loss of limbs and life experienced far too often by our courageous military personnel. Army wife

By Dawn's Early Light

Kim Miller shared, "We lost a very dear friend, someone my husband had served with on his first deployment to Iraq, shortly after they redeployed." Kim and her family were shocked. They had just seen their friend shortly before the terrible accident. "He was killed in a helicopter accident, and there was a certain amount of disbelief in the whole thing." No one expected such a tragedy after this man had already made it home from his first deployment in Iraq. "These guys had been to Iraq, at the ugly beginning of the war, and they had come home. They were supposed to be safe." That's what they all believed—that they would be safe. "It was a terrible time for our friend's widow and family, for our tight-knit group of friends, for the unit they had served with," Kim shared. The reality of war and loss of life came crashing down on her and her family.

"It was very eye-opening, too, for us as a young Army family and really drove home some of the difficult realities of military life." For certain, war changes people. Everyone affiliated with military life will be changed. Loss of friends and family will never be easy. But, in such times, our faith rises to the occasion. We pray, we act from our hearts—we spread Christ's love.

Kim recalled that, as hard as it was to lose their friend, "it also taught us many good lessons about what to do in that situation—a situation that unfortunately in the military can and does happen too often." She added, "We all did our best, I think, given the situation, but there were times when we weren't sure how best to grieve with, and how best to be there for our friend." Adding to that, Kim recollected, "It's not a time I'd like to go back to, but I hope that the lessons we learned during that tough time will make me a more compassionate, caring person every day of my life."

Suicide

I know more than a few families who have lost loved ones through suicide—some because of the pressures and torments of war. Suicide is a sorrowful subject indeed, but nonetheless an important one. It affects not only the person who committed suicide but also the countless people who knew that person. As well, it can cause confusion, regret, distress, and even feelings of guilt in those who are shocked upon hearing the news and might immediately question whether they could have done something to prevent the sorrowful and unchangeable act.

The Church teaches that we should not take our own lives, that it is a grave sin as taught in the Fifth Commandment. The *Catechism* says:

> Everyone is responsible for his life before God who has given it to him. It is God who remains the sovereign Master of life. We are obliged to accept life gratefully and preserve it for his honor and the salvation of our souls. We are stewards, not owners, of the life God has entrusted to us. It is not ours to dispose of. (2280)

But we must remember that the Church also tells us that, in some cases, suicide is not a mortal sin because the person who committed suicide might not have been in his or her right mind. The *Catechism* states:

> Grave psychological disturbances, anguish, or grave fear of hardship, suffering, or torture can diminish the responsibility of the one committing suicide. We should not despair of the eternal salvation of persons who have taken their own lives. By ways known to him alone, God can provide the opportunity for salutary repentance. The

By Dawn's Early Light

Church prays for persons who have taken their own lives.
(2282–2283)

Let us continue to pray for the souls of the dead and to have great hope in God's everlasting mercy.

One young man from a family I know committed suicide after placing a rosary around his neck, seemingly hoping for protection and help from the Blessed Mother during the act of ending his life. He seemed to desire God's mercy. We can never assume to know or understand what might have been going through a suicidal person's mind or what it was that drove him or her to despair before committing the act. Nor should we ever judge another's heart and soul. We won't know this side of Heaven how the person's mind might have changed before he or she died.

We can be encouraged, recalling St. Faustina's words in her *Diary* with regard to God's mercy for a soul who is at the point of death. She wrote:

> God's mercy sometimes touches the sinner at the last moment in a wondrous and mysterious way. Outwardly, it seems as if everything were lost, but it is not so. The soul, illumined by a ray of God's powerful final grace, turns to God in the last moment with such a power of love that, in an instant, it receives from God forgiveness of sin and punishment, while outwardly it shows no sign either of repentance or of contrition, because souls [at that stage] no longer react to external things. Oh, how beyond comprehension is God's mercy! But—horror!—there are also souls who voluntarily and consciously reject and scorn this grace! Although a person is at the point of death, the merciful God gives the soul that interior vivid

242

moment, so that if the soul is willing, it has the possibility of returning to God.[76]

For some individuals, military pressures and stresses can be too much to bear, especially in those who have witnessed the horrors of war. Are we doing enough to aid our soldiers to transition back to life after deployments? I certainly do not think so. Moreover, how can we comfort the families of suicide victims? One way is to express our sorrow, to arrange holy Masses to be said for the person whose life was lost, to promise our prayers, to give hugs, and to stay in touch with the heartbroken family who will need continual encouragement and support.

> "I can do all things through Christ
> who strengthens me."
>
> —Philippians 4:13

This Valley of Tears

I vividly recall my mother's tears for my two brothers away in Vietnam. She was so concerned for their safety and would pray intensely while crying. I also remember my older brother crying one time. It was the only time I had ever seen my stoic brother shed a tear. It was at the funeral Mass of a soldier who had taken his life through suicide. At times like these, we can recall the line in the Hail, Holy Queen: "To thee do we send up our sighs, mourning, and weeping in this valley of tears." This life on earth is a valley of tears, but we also possess a deep and abiding joy and great hope, knowing that there is an eternal life that follows this one.

[76] *Diary of Saint Maria Faustina Kowalska*, 1698.

There are many hidden tears associated with military life. Sometimes we cry inside, wanting to put up a good exterior in order to help family members around us. Other times our tears are out in the open, and there is sometimes the need to cry on someone's shoulder, perhaps during deployments or losses. We can console one another with our warm embrace, Christ's love radiating through us.

Carrying our cross through tears can be extremely difficult at times, especially when it is related to the loss of life we might experience as part of the military family. Thomas à Kempis tells us: "If you carry your cross willingly, it will carry and lead you to the desired goal where indeed there shall be no more suffering, but here there shall be. If you carry it unwillingly, you create a burden for yourself and increase the load, though still you have to bear it. If you cast away one cross, you will find another, perhaps a heavier one."[77]

Jesus tells us that He will wipe every tear from our eyes. "Death will be no more; mourning and crying and pain will be no more, for the first things have passed away. And the one who was seated on the throne said, 'See, I am making all things new'" (Rev. 21:4–5).

[77] Thomas à Kempis, *The Imitation of Christ*, 2, 12.

Hail, Holy Queen

Hail, Holy Queen, Mother of Mercy,
hail, our life, our sweetness and our hope.

To thee do we cry, poor banished children of Eve:
to thee do we send up our sighs,
mourning, and weeping
in this valley of tears.

Turn then, most gracious advocate,
thine eyes of mercy toward us,
and after this our exile,
show unto us
the blessed fruit
of thy womb, Jesus.

O merciful,
O loving,
O sweet Virgin Mary!

Divine Mercy for Soldiers

"Blessed are the merciful, for they shall obtain mercy" (Matt. 5:7). St. Faustina, the great apostle of mercy, wrote about the importance of praying for others and our responsibility in helping their souls, while making an analogy to soldiers fighting a war. She wrote in her *Diary*, "As God has made us sharers in his mercy and even more than that, dispensers of that mercy, we should therefore have great love for each soul, beginning with the elect and ending with the soul that does not yet know God." She continued, "By prayer and mortification, we will make our way to the most uncivilized countries, paving the way for the missionaries." Then she drives home her message: "We will bear in mind that a soldier on the front lines cannot hold out long without support from the rear forces that do not actually take part in the fighting but provide for all his needs; and that such is the role of prayer, and that therefore each one of us is to be distinguished by an apostolic spirit."[78]

Speaking of Divine Mercy, Air Force wife Aimee Miller shared that she is strengthened by the unknown because it prods her to trust God with her life and the lives of her family members. She explained, "It is incredibly hard not to know what your future holds, and it really makes you rely on God and believe what the image of Divine Mercy tells us to pray: 'Jesus, I trust in you.'"

We need to trust God with all aspects of our lives. Learning about Divine Mercy can greatly help us to do just that.

Marine wife Linda Bontempo Coleman reflected on her trust in God's great mercy. She shared with me, "After five years of struggling with infertility and the grief of many miscarriages, my husband, Larry, and I welcomed our first child just a couple

---

[78] *Diary of Saint Maria Faustina Kowalska*, 230.

of days before Christmas 2002." This couple couldn't be more
overjoyed. But then, "Less than a month later, Larry deployed
for Operation Iraqi Freedom."

As a brand-new mother, Linda needed to adjust quickly to
just about everything that parenting a newborn entailed and to
pray to be able to handle it on her own. She was deeply thankful
for the gift of their child and needed to trust firmly in her Lord.
Explaining the military operation, Linda recalled, "This was the
first wave, and our Marines experienced intense fighting in the
spring of 2003." She focused on her precious baby and prayed
intensely for her husband and all of the others in the battalion.
"While I did miss him," Linda shared, "I rarely worried about
him. Not only did I know just how well trained our battalion
was, but more importantly, I was blessed with an overwhelming
sense that God had this. God would provide—and in my mind,
that meant He had a plan for my little family."

Linda would continue to trust and pray. "I trusted God to see
us through this deployment, through the first months of being a
new mom without my husband, and to take care of my Marine.
I trusted God to bring Larry back home to us."

Although Linda trusted in God with all her heart and hoped
against all hope, she shared, "I wasn't naive enough to believe
that there wouldn't be casualties and deaths." But they had been
through so much already, Linda felt a strong need to trust God
and hope for the very best. "I just believed that God hadn't
brought us through the past five years of heartache, just to take
Larry, the father of my newborn baby, away from us while deployed to a combat zone." She added, "I trusted my belief that
God would *always* provide for me."

There's something about babies and deployments! Later, in
February 2005, Linda and Larry found out through an ultrasound

that Linda was carrying quadruplets! Linda recalled, "The next day Larry was deploying again to Iraq. This time it was supposed to be for fourteen months." Can you imagine what it was like for Linda and Larry to receive that order of deployment, with four babies on the way, and knowing they'd be in for such a long haul? And on top of that, this military couple had a thirteen-month-old. Linda said, "Thanks to a wonderful battalion commanding officer, Larry was brought home after only a few months," adding that it was perfect timing—"just as I was being put on full bed rest at home."

Recalling the pain of her losses and reflecting on God's amazing plans, Linda said, "When Larry deployed, my first thoughts were, 'I've miscarried so many times before, including single babies and twins; how am I going to carry four babies while taking care of a thirteen-month-old?'" But, Linda's heart knew. "Again, I had to trust that God would provide. I trusted I would find the support I would need in our Marine Corps community, and I trusted that God would bring Larry home safely." Brimming with joy, she added, "God provided!"

Divine Mercy Message

The Divine Mercy message is completely rooted in Scripture. God's love has always been forgiving and merciful. "But in the Divine Mercy devotion, the message takes on a powerful new focus, calling people to a deeper understanding that God's love is unlimited and available to everyone—especially the greatest sinners."[79]

[79] "Background of the Divine Mercy Devotion," EWTN, https://www.ewtn.com/devotionals/mercy/backgr.htm.

Out of obedience to her spiritual director, Sister Faustina wrote in a diary the occurrences, visions, and Jesus' words to her. She recalled the details of the vision of God's mercy in her *Diary*:

I saw a great light, with God the Father in the midst of it. Between this light and the earth I saw Jesus nailed to the Cross and in such a way that God, wanting to look upon the earth, had to look through Our Lord's wounds and I understood that God blessed the earth for the sake of Jesus.[80]

Sister Faustina wrote about another vision she received on September 13, 1935:

I saw an angel, the executor of God's wrath … about to strike the earth.… I began to beg God earnestly for the world with words which I heard interiorly. As I prayed in this way, I saw the angel's helplessness, and he could not carry out the just punishment.[81]

The following day she learned through an inner voice how to pray the prayer on rosary beads.

[80] "The Chaplet of Divine Mercy," EWTN, https://www.ewtn.com/devotionals/mercy/dmmap.htm.
[81] Ibid.

By Dawn's Early Light

The Divine Mercy Chaplet

Many Catholics pray the Divine Mercy Chaplet each day, when they can, at 3:00 p.m., the Hour of Great Mercy. Another important time to pray the Chaplet is at the bedside of a dying person or for a dying person wherever he or she may be. You can also pray the Chaplet for all people who will die that day or night.

The Divine Mercy Chaplet may be prayed using rosary beads.

1. *Begin with the Sign of the Cross, one Our Father, one Hail Mary, and the Apostles' Creed.*

2. *On the Our Father beads, pray the following:*
   Eternal Father,
   I offer you the Body and Blood, Soul and Divinity
   of your dearly beloved Son, Our Lord Jesus Christ,
   in atonement for our sins and those of the whole world.

3. *On each of the Hail Mary beads, pray the following:*
   For the sake of His sorrowful Passion,
   have mercy on us and on the whole world.

   Repeat steps 2 and 3 for all five decades.

4. *Pray the following prayer three times:*
   Holy God, Holy Mighty One, Holy Immortal One,
   have mercy on us and on the whole world.

5. *Conclude with the Sign of the Cross.*

Jesus later instructed Sister Faustina:

Say unceasingly this chaplet that I have taught you. Anyone who says it will receive great Mercy at the hour of death. Priests will recommend it to sinners as the last hope. Even the most hardened sinner, if he recites this Chaplet even once, will receive grace from My Infinite Mercy. I want the whole world to know My Infinite Mercy. I want to give unimaginable graces to those who trust in My Mercy.

When they say this chaplet in the presence of the dying, I will stand between My Father and the dying person not as the just judge but as the Merciful Savior.[82]

The priests of the Congregation of Marians of the Immaculate Conception in Stockbridge, Massachusetts, instruct the faithful to believe and trust in God's mercy and to show mercy to others. They explain that God's mercy is greater than our sins—always. God wants us to call upon His mercy with great trust. He wants us to allow His mercy to flow through us to others, and in that way we all experience the great joy of God. The Marians recommend calling to mind the letters ABC to live the Divine Mercy message:

A — Ask for His mercy. God wants us to approach Him in prayer constantly, repenting of our sins and asking Him to pour His mercy out upon us and upon the whole world.

B — Be merciful. God wants us to receive His mercy and let it flow through us to others. He wants us to extend love and forgiveness to others, just as He does to us.

C — Completely trust in Jesus. God wants us to know that the graces of His mercy are dependent upon our trust. The more we trust in Jesus, the more we will receive.[83]

[82] Ibid.
[83] "Background of the Divine Mercy Devotion."

A Prayer of Divine Mercy

O greatly merciful God, infinite Goodness,
today all mankind calls out from the abyss
of its misery to Your mercy—to Your compassion.

O God, it is with its mighty voice
of misery that it cries out.

Gracious God, do not reject the prayer
of this earth's exiles!

O Lord, goodness beyond our understanding,
who are acquainted with our misery
through and through,
and know that by our own power
we cannot ascend to You,
we implore You: anticipate us with Your Grace
and keep increasing Your mercy in us,
that we may faithfully do Your holy will
all through our life and at death's hour.

Let the omnipotence of Your mercy
shield us from the darts of our salvation's enemies,
that we may with confidence,
as Your children await Your final coming
on that day known to You alone.

And we expect to obtain everything promised us
by Jesus in spite of all our wretchedness.

For Jesus is our hope: Through His merciful heart
as through an open gate we pass through to Heaven.[84]

[84] *Diary of Saint Maria Faustina Kowalska*, 1570.

Prayer to Our Lady of Sorrows

O Mother of Sorrows, who could express the cruel anguish of this moment?

The same child whom you wrapped in swaddling clothes amidst unspeakable joy, you now wrap silently in the burial shroud.

Your tears mingle with the blood and dirt that covers His broken body.

But even in this moment your trust in His promise did not die. Your mourning was not without hope, for you knew that He would rise again from His grave, just as He promised.

Through this bitter sword obtain for us the grace to believe with unshakable hope in the victory of our Lord, even in the darkest moments of life. Amen.

To You, O Lord, I Lift Up My Soul

We've discussed the pain of loss of cherished neighbors through deployments, loss of life in the military, sorrowful suicide, trusting in God's Divine Mercy, and more. Take some time to ponder God speaking to your heart. Can you trust His great and unfathomable mercy for you? Can you commit to more times of prayer throughout your busy days? Try your best to offer your heart to God throughout each day and offer your care of those "under your command" to God's great mercy.

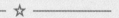

Prayer of Trust in God's Mercy

Every day, new challenges surface
and will continue to do so.

Such is life.

Every day, I want to renew
my hope in You, my God.

You love me more
than I can understand.

Jesus, I trust in You! Amen.

11

Ask for Hope and Endurance

But I will hope continually.

—Psalm 71:14

In his Encyclical Letter *Spe Salvi*, Pope Emeritus Benedict XVI wrote about Francis Xavier Nguyen Van Thuan:

> The late Cardinal Nguyen Van Thuan, a prisoner for thirteen years, nine of them spent in solitary confinement, has left us a precious little book: *Prayers of Hope*. During thirteen years in jail, in a situation of seemingly utter hopelessness, the fact that he could listen and speak to God became for him an increasing power of hope, which enabled him, after his release, to become for people all over the world a witness of hope — to that great hope which does not wane even in the nights of solitude.[85]

Witness of Hope and Joy

After his imprisonment, Cardinal Nguyen Van Thuan served as vice president and then president of the Pontifical Council for Justice and Peace and was named a cardinal in 2001. He died the following year. During his imprisonment, this saintly man clandestinely offered daily private holy Masses using the palm of his hand as a chalice for the Precious Blood and using bread and wine that were smuggled in to him as "medicine for his stomach."

[85] *Saved in Hope: Encyclical Letter of the Supreme Pontiff Benedict XVI* (San Francisco: Ignatius Press, 2008), 32.

He secretly ordained priests, distributed Communion to Catholic prisoners, and converted Buddhists and atheists who had been curious as to why he radiated joy.

Just days after his death the *Telegraph* reported on his life. Here is an excerpt:

> Every night he ripped a page from his calendar and penciled a thought in Italian on the back. Children playing nearby would pass on the notes to local Roman Catholics. In return, Thuan would be sent food packages, wrapped in the pages of the Vatican newspaper, *L'Osservatore Romano*, which had been declared illegal by the Communist regime.... Thuan managed to say Mass every day of his imprisonment, including during his nine years of solitary confinement. The Communists noted Thuan's habit of evangelizing his goalers, and at first changed his guards every 15 days; but this became too expensive. He taught his warders pidgin French and English, and persuaded them to give him a strip of electric wire and piece of wood, which he fashioned into a pectoral cross and chain that he concealed in a sliver of soap. On his release Thuan wore it openly, proclaiming the cross a sign of "the love of Jesus."[86]

"Hope does not disappoint, because the love of God has been poured out into our hearts through the Holy Spirit" (Rom. 5:5, NABRE). Cardinal Nguyen Van Thuan's witness and life of hope despite great hardship are incredible examples of holiness and

---

[86] "Cardinal Nguyen Van Thuan," *Telegraph*, http://www.telegraph. co.uk/news/obituaries/1407591/Cardinal-Nguyen-Van-Thuan. html.

heroic virtue. While he was in prison, he received permission to write things down, for he felt inspired to record his thoughts and prayers. In one such reflection on prayer, he wrote, "Prayer is the breath of the soul. Without prayer, the soul suffocates." He continued, "Through prayer, I live in you, Lord. I live in you as a baby in its mother's womb with its breath united to hers and its heart beating in rhythm with hers."[87]

The Ship of Life
St. Basil the Great (329–379)

Steer the ship of my life, good Lord,
to your quiet harbor, where I can be safe
from the storms of sin and conflict.

Show me the course I should take.
Renew in me the gift of discernment,
so that I can always see
the right direction in which I should go.

Give me the strength
and the courage to choose the right course,
even when the sea is rough
and the waves are high,
knowing that through
enduring hardship and danger,
in Your name, we shall find
comfort and peace. Amen.

[87] Nguyễn, *Prayers of Hope, Words of Courage*, 114.

By Dawn's Early Light

Litany of the Saints

The Litany of the Saints is a powerful prayer. It can be prayed for someone in danger of death. It is also prayed at the Easter Vigil, at Baptisms, and at Ordinations. It may be prayed alone or in a group. I suggest that families pray it together before deployments.

Lord, have mercy on us.

Christ, have mercy on us.

Lord, have mercy on us.

Christ, hear us.

Christ, graciously hear us.

God the Father of Heaven, *have mercy on us.*

God the Son, Redeemer of the world, *have mercy on us.*

God the Holy Spirit, *have mercy on us.*

Holy Trinity, one God, *have mercy on us.*

Holy Mary, *pray for us* [or *him* or *her*].

Holy Mother of God, *pray for us.*

Holy Virgin of virgins, *pray for us.*

St. Michael, *pray for us.*

St. Gabriel, *pray for us.*

St. Raphael, *pray for us.*

All you holy angels and archangels, *pray for us.*

All you holy orders of blessed spirits, *pray for us.*

St. John the Baptist, *pray for us.*

St. Joseph, *pray for us.*

All you holy patriarchs and prophets, *pray for us.*

St. Peter, *pray for us.*

St. Paul, *pray for us.*

St. Andrew, *pray for us.*

St. James, *pray for us.*

St. John, *pray for us.*

St. Thomas, *pray for us.*

St. James, *pray for us.*
St. Philip, *pray for us.*
St. Bartholomew, *pray for us.*
St. Matthew, *pray for us.*
St. Simon, *pray for us.*
St. Thaddeus, *pray for us.*
St. Matthias, *pray for us.*
St. Barnabas, *pray for us.*
St. Luke, *pray for us.*
St. Mark, *pray for us.*
All you holy apostles and evangelists, *pray for us.*
All you holy disciples of our Lord, *pray for us.*
All you holy innocents, *pray for us.*
St. Stephen, *pray for us.*
St. Lawrence, *pray for us.*
St. Vincent, *pray for us.*
Sts. Fabian and Sebastian, *pray for us.*
Sts. John and Paul, *pray for us.*
Sts. Cosmas and Damian, *pray for us.*
Sts. Gervase and Protase, *pray for us.*
All you holy martyrs, *pray for us.*
St. Sylvester, *pray for us.*
St. Gregory, *pray for us.*
St. Ambrose, *pray for us.*
St. Augustine, *pray for us.*
St. Jerome, *pray for us.*
St. Martin, *pray for us.*
St. Nicholas, *pray for us.*
All you holy bishops and confessors, *pray for us.*
All you holy doctors, *pray for us.*
St. Anthony, *pray for us.*

By Dawn's Early Light

St. Benedict, *pray for us.*
St. Bernard, *pray for us.*
St. Dominic, *pray for us.*
St. Francis, *pray for us.*
All you holy priests and levites, *pray for us.*
All you holy monks and hermits, *pray for us.*
St. Mary Magdalen, *pray for us.*
St. Agatha, *pray for us.*
St. Lucy, *pray for us.*
St. Agnes, *pray for us.*
St. Cecilia, *pray for us.*
St. Catherine, *pray for us.*
St. Anastasia, *pray for us.*
All you holy virgins and widows, *pray for us.*
All you holy men and women, saints of God,
    intercede for us.
Be merciful, *spare us, O Lord.*
Be merciful, *graciously hear us, O Lord.*
From all evil, *deliver us, O Lord.*
From all sin, *deliver us, O Lord.*
From Thy wrath, *deliver us, O Lord.*
From a sudden and unprovided death, *deliver us,*
    O Lord.
From the deceits of the devil, *deliver us, O Lord.*
From anger, and hatred, and all ill will, *deliver us,*
    O Lord.
From the spirit of fornication, *deliver us, O Lord.*
From lightning and tempest, *deliver us, O Lord.*
From the scourge of earthquakes, *deliver us, O Lord.*
From plague, famine and war, *deliver us, O Lord.*
From everlasting death, *deliver us, O Lord.*

By the mystery of Thy holy Incarnation, *deliver us,*
    O Lord.
By Thy coming, *deliver us, O Lord.*
By Thy nativity, *deliver us, O Lord.*
By Thy baptism and holy fasting, *deliver us, O Lord.*
By Thy Cross and Passion, *deliver us, O Lord.*
By Thy death and burial, *deliver us, O Lord.*
By Thy holy Resurrection, *deliver us, O Lord.*
By Thine admirable Ascension, *deliver us, O Lord.*
By the coming of the Holy Spirit, the Paraclete, *deliver*
    us, O Lord.
On the day of judgment, *deliver us, O Lord.*
We sinners, *we beseech Thee, hear us.*
That Thou wouldst spare us, *we beseech Thee, hear us.*
That Thou wouldst pardon us, *we beseech Thee, hear us.*
That Thou wouldst bring us to true penance, *we*
    beseech Thee, hear us.
That Thou wouldst vouchsafe to govern and preserve
    Thy Holy Church, *we beseech Thee, hear us.*
That Thou wouldst vouchsafe to preserve our
    Apostolic Prelate and all ecclesiastical orders in
    holy religion, *we beseech Thee, hear us.*
That Thou wouldst vouchsafe to humble the enemies
    of holy Church, *we beseech Thee, hear us.*
That Thou wouldst vouchsafe to give peace and true
    concord to Christian kings and princes, *we beseech*
    Thee, hear us.
That Thou wouldst vouchsafe to grant peace and unity
    to all Christian peoples, *we beseech Thee, hear us.*
That Thou wouldst vouchsafe to bring back to the
    unity of the Church all who have strayed away, and

lead to the light of the Gospel all unbelievers, *we beseech Thee, hear us.*

That Thou wouldst vouchsafe to confirm and preserve us in Thy holy service, *we beseech Thee, hear us.*

That Thou wouldst lift our minds to heavenly desires, *we beseech Thee, hear us.*

That Thou wouldst render eternal blessings to all our benefactors, *we beseech Thee, hear us.*

That Thou wouldst deliver our souls, and the souls of our brethren, relatives, and benefactors from eternal damnation, *we beseech Thee, hear us.*

That Thou wouldst vouchsafe to give and preserve the fruits of the earth, *we beseech Thee, hear us.*

That Thou wouldst vouchsafe to grant eternal rest to all the faithful departed, *we beseech Thee, hear us.*

That Thou wouldst vouchsafe graciously to hear us, Son of God, *we beseech Thee, hear us.*

Lamb of God who takest away the sins of the world, *spare us, O Lord.*

Lamb of God, who takest away the sins of the world, *graciously hear us, O Lord.*

Lamb of God, who takest away the sins of the world, *have mercy on us.*

Christ, hear us.

Christ, graciously hear us.

Lord, have mercy on us.

Christ, have mercy on us.

Lord, have mercy on us.

Our Father ... (*inaudibly*) and lead us not into temptation, but deliver us from evil. Amen.

Pope John Paul II's Message of Peace

The heart of the Gospel message is Christ, who is everyone's peace and reconciliation. May his countenance
shine upon the path of humanity as it prepares to cross
the threshold of the Third Millennium!

May his justice and his peace become a gift for all,
without distinction!
"Then shall the wilderness be fertile land
and fertile land become forest.
In the wilderness justice will come to live,
and integrity in the fertile land;
integrity will bring peace,
justice give everlasting security." (Isa. 32:15–17)[88]

Psalm 43

Grant me justice, O God;
  defend me from a faithless people;
  from the deceitful and unjust rescue me.
You, O God, are my strength.
  Why then do you spurn me?
Why must I go about mourning,
  with the enemy oppressing me?
Send your light and your fidelity,
  that they may be my guide;

---

[88] John Paul II, Message for the Celebration of the World Day of
Peace (December 8, 1997), no. 9.

By Dawn's Early Light

Let them bring me to your holy mountain,
to the place of your dwelling,
That I may come to the altar of God,
to God, my joy, my delight.
Then I will praise you with the harp,
O God, my God.
Why are you downcast, my soul?
Why do you groan within me?
Wait for God, for I shall again praise him,
my savior and my God.

Praying You Home!

I place my hope and trust in You,
O Lord, that You will bring my soldier
back home to me.

Please comfort my worried heart
and dry my many tears.
Please bring my soldier home! Amen.

All Things Are Possible

Love feels no burden,
thinks nothing of its trouble,
attempts what is above its strength,
pleads no excuse for impossibility,

for it thinks all things are lawful for itself
and all things are possible.

Putting Down Roots and Tearing Them Up

Lord, it's so hard to start all over again
after just getting established at another location.
I feel as if I just put down new roots
only to tear them up all over again.

It's also extremely painful
to bid my soldier goodbye when
he gets his orders for deployment.

These changes weigh immensely
on my sometimes fragile heart.

Please give me strength and courage
to carry on in faith
and to know that You are
with us every step of the way. Amen.

Psalm 42

As the deer longs for streams of water,
so my soul longs for you, O God.
My soul thirsts for God, the living God.
When can I enter and see the face of God?
My tears have been my bread day and night,
as they ask me every day, "Where is your God?"
Those times I recall

By Dawn's Early Light

as I pour out my soul,
When I would cross over to the shrine of the Mighty One,
    to the house of God,
Amid loud cries of thanksgiving,
    with the multitude keeping festival.
Why are you downcast, my soul;
    why do you groan within me?
Wait for God, for I shall again praise him,
    my savior and my God.
My soul is downcast within me;
    therefore I remember you
From the land of the Jordan and Hermon,
    from Mount Mizar,
Deep calls to deep
    in the roar of your torrents,
    and all your waves and breakers
    sweep over me.
By day may the LORD send his mercy,
    and by night may his righteousness be with me!
    I will pray to the God of my life,
I will say to God, my rock:
    "Why do you forget me?
Why must I go about mourning
    with the enemy oppressing me?"
It shatters my bones, when my adversaries reproach me,
    when they say to me every day: "Where is your God?"
Why are you downcast, my soul,
    why do you groan within me?
Wait for God, for I shall again praise him,
    my savior and my God.

Ask for Hope and Endurance

Waiting on the Lord

It's hard to wait for the Lord to answer your prayers, or to wait for anything, for that matter, especially since we live in such a fast-paced world filled with ever-changing technology. We are quite accustomed to instant gratification with regard to status updates on our smartphones and through social media. But God tells us, "Be still and know that I am God" (Ps. 46:11). Can we be still? Is it possible? Even for a little while? Sometimes, we receive a yes or a no as an answer to our pleas to God. Sometimes it is a "wait and be still." Our Lord is the Divine Physician and knows just what we need and when we need it.

Speaking of waiting, one time my doctor ordered me to stay still for almost a full nine months! That was due to a precarious pregnancy in which I had a heart condition and a hemorrhaged uterus. Nine months is an awful lot of waiting on the Lord. Yet every one of my multiple ultrasounds confirmed a beating heart and a growing baby, albeit a pool of blood in my uterus not yet resolved. I had to stay still and off my feet, for the most part, and continue to trust God. I am deeply grateful that both my unborn baby and I survived that pregnancy.

Army wife Kim Miller confessed, "Like a lot of people, I like to feel in control." Then she chuckled. "Military life definitely requires you to give a lot of control over to things way outside your influence. Deployments and the fact that my husband puts his life on the line are scary, but those are temporary situations." Kim is referring to the fact that there is so much about the military that is uncertain. One grows closer to God in those uncertainties when one seeks Him first and foremost. Kim added, "I think the continual lack of control over a lot of parts of your life is a much scarier aspect of military life."

By Dawn's Early Light

Kim reflected on the past fifteen years of military service. She shared, "After I joined the Military Council of Catholic Women, so many opportunities to learn about and grow in my Faith were made available to me." Further, she said, "I think that this path is one that God set me on and I have just had to be open to it to see all the goodness He can do in my life. This isn't to say that I am living a saintly life each and every moment of every day," she quipped, "but being open to His grace and reflective about where I am in my journey of faith has made it easier to see all the times He has had a hand in my life."

Finally, reflecting on how her life has changed during the military years, she shared about the amazing blessing of friendships. "The friendships we have forged are the most profound part of our experience as a military family. My husband and I marvel at the interconnected web of relationships that span, if not the world, definitely the United States," she said. "When we travel as a family we are never far from a friend, and anytime we move, we look forward to catching up with friends stationed at or near our new duty station."

Keeping Your Soldier Close

It is extremely hard to wait for your soldier to come back home. Added to that is the constant worry about their safety and well-being. Army wife Diane Joyce Bridon shared with me some ways that her family keeps the family united and their soldier close. She said, "In our house, we did not allow any deployments to become negative, even though it was a very sad situation." Her family has always rallied together to do all they could to shore up her husband. It was sad for them to see him go, but Diane explained, "Once he was gone, we concentrated on supporting him, keeping everything going at home so he could focus on the mission at hand." They didn't want him to worry about them back home. They would hang in there for him. "We would have fun making a themed box with all kinds of goodies and treats once a month to send to him. One time we had cobwebs all throughout the box with spiders, and treats, and funny items for the month of October." She added, "He always looked forward to them."

Diane and her children found a way to keep their Sunday family dinners alive, even though their soldier was deployed. "We had dinner on Skype [video-conferencing] every Sunday, even if it was early in the afternoon for us." They didn't worry about the time difference. They made it work! "We would gather at the dinner table with our meals. Dan picked up food and we spent an hour or more together to continue family dinner time talks even while he was deployed," Diane explained.

Prayer for Peace
St. John of the Cross (1542–1591)

O blessed Jesus,
give me stillness of soul in You.
Let Your mighty calmness reign in me.
Rule me, O King of Gentleness,
King of Peace. Amen.

By Dawn's Early Light

Seeking God's Will
Psalm 27:7–9, 13–14

Hear, O LORD, when I cry aloud,
  be gracious to me and answer me!
"Come," my heart says, "seek his face!"
  Your face, LORD, do I seek.
Do not hide your face from me....
I believe that I shall see the goodness of the LORD
  in the land of the living.
Wait for the LORD;
  be strong, and let your heart take courage;
  wait for the LORD! (RSVCE)

A Prayer to Desire What Pleases God
St. Thomas Aquinas (1225–1274)

Grant me grace,
O merciful God,
to desire ardently
all that is pleasing to You,
to examine it prudently,
to acknowledge it truthfully,
and to accomplish it perfectly,
for the praise and glory of Your name. Amen.

Ask for Hope and Endurance

Matthew 5:11-12

Blessed are you when men revile you and persecute you and utter all kinds of evil against you falsely on my account. Rejoice and be glad, for your reward is great in heaven.

For a Holy Death
Blessed John Henry Newman (1801–1890)

May the Lord support us all day long,
'til the shadows lengthen
and the evening comes,
and the busy world is hushed,
and the fever of life is over,
and our work is done.

Then in His mercy
may He give us a safe lodging,
and a holy rest, and peace at last. Amen.

Prayer to St. Joseph for a Happy Death
O Blessed Joseph,
who died in the arms of Jesus and Mary,
obtain for me, I beseech you,
the grace of a happy death.

By Dawn's Early Light

In that hour of dread and anguish,
assist me by your presence,
and protect me by your power
against the enemies of my salvation.

Into your sacred hands,
living and dying,
Jesus, Mary, Joseph,
I commend my soul. Amen.

Prayer for Someone Deceased

Eternal rest grant unto him/her, O Lord,
and let perpetual light shine upon him/her.
May he/she rest in peace. Amen.

May his/her soul and the souls
of all the faithful departed,
through the mercy of God,
rest in peace. Amen.

To You, O Lord, I Lift Up My Soul

This chapter has spoken about hopeful endurance during times of uncertainty and difficulties. We discussed waiting on the Lord, growing in faith, and keeping your soldier close even through deployments, among other things. Can you take some time to reflect on our Lord in your life? Do you try to be still at times and acknowledge God present in that moment of your day? Try to find more moments to pause and, as our Lord instructs, "Be still and know that I am God" (Ps. 46:11). These simple prayerful acts can bring hope to your heart.

———— ☆ ————

Prayer to Be a Light to Others

Protect us,
O Lord, we pray.

Please, Lord, help me to be a light
to others who are struggling along
to find the way that leads to You. Amen.

12

Express Gratitude

Draw near to God, and he will draw near to you.

—James 4:8, NABRE

In keeping a continual conversation of prayer with our Lord, we want to be sure that we are not simply beseeching God with all of our petitions. We want to make sure that we frequently thank Him for His many blessings first before we start petitioning for "things" we need or think we need. In fact, Mother Teresa has taught, "Prayer is not asking. Prayer is putting oneself in the hands of God, at His disposition, and listening to His voice in the depths of our hearts."

My husband, Dave, recalls that, at a family gathering, my brother Tim, who fought in the Vietnam War, had said, "There are no atheists in a foxhole." It's something to think about. Do we suddenly find the need to call upon God or acknowledge him only when it is a matter of life and death?

Many of the saints have taught us the importance of prayer and that it needs to be ongoing. Recall that Cardinal Francis Xavier Nguyen Van Thuan wrote that "prayer is the breath of the soul. Without prayer, the soul suffocates." A very vivid image indeed. Do we care for our prayer lives to make sure our souls are "breathing"? St. John Paul II said, "In prayer you become one with the source of our true light—Jesus Himself."

By Dawn's Early Light

Thank You for Sticking with Me, Lord

Dear Lord,
I can never thank You enough
for always sticking with me
even though I do not always stick with You.

Please strengthen me
on my journey
so that I will never
turn my back on You! Amen.

An Army Wife Reflects

Army wife Michelle Nash shared some of her military journey with me. "My Army-spouse journey began in March of 1995 when I said my own fiat to my husband. Really, I had no idea of what that 'fiat' meant for my service to our Lord through this channel of selfless service to His chosen military families and to my own." Along the way, Michelle would learn more about what that meant, but she and her husband, Kevin, needed to establish some parameters. She said, "Raising four children and keeping them in an environment of constant change meant for our family that we needed to stand firm in our nonnegotiables as parents and as a military family. No excuses!" Michelle shared those "nonnegotiables" with me. She and her husband made sure they always attended Mass together and prayed as a family each night, and she explained, "We will never allow the things we don't have to cause us to be ungrateful for the things we do have. If Dad ever has to miss Christmas, we always open our gifts when we are together again as family!"

Michelle explained the constant need for prayer and God in her life. "The military life has afforded me many opportunities where the only constants in my day-to-day life were God and prayer." She also recalled the painful waiting for her soldier to come home. "I have often lived much like a prisoner, counting down time and days when I could be reunited with my husband." She added, "The distance was always the great trial in my day-to-day life."

Michelle feels the need to pray for her soldier and other soldiers. In addition, she has been instrumental in leading other military women in the Faith in her many roles, including serving as a CWOC president for four military chapel installations, as the MCCW Southeast Regional Coordinator, and as the MCCW Pacific Regional Coordinator. At the writing of this book, she holds the position of the MCCW Worldwide President. Michelle shared, "I often tell my husband that, while he is the active-duty soldier, I am a soldier in the *Army of God* and my general has way more power than his ever will." Michelle is grateful for those she has met and has come close to in her military journey thus far. "The military lifestyle has given me my best friends, a family I have chosen." She added, "The Lord has allowed me to have 'a service within a service,' and I could not be more willing to put faith into action than as a military spouse."

A Loss of Life, a Letter, and an Unforgettable Friendship

Michelle Nash shared with me a moving story about an experience that impacted her life. Her husband, Kevin, was stationed in Korea at the time. Just two days before a young soldier was due to go home, a devastating accident occurred. "A tank rolled over his billet and killed the sleeping soldier." Michelle said, "My husband was in charge of contacting the family of this nineteen-year-old: his spouse, who was pregnant with their first child, and his parents." But Michelle knew nothing about this awful casualty because, she said, "my husband was trying to keep my stress down."

Then Michelle received a letter from the widow of the deceased soldier. Michelle explained, "My husband told her to contact me stateside if there was anything she needed prior to her husband's body returning. We were both due, she in August and I in July, with our first children."

"The letter moved me to tears because she was thanking me, believe it or not, in her circumstances—thanking me for the check she received in the mail from my husband with a card from both of us for baby items she might need until her insurance money was received from the life-insurance settlement." Michelle said, "I burst into tears." She decided to call the grieving woman. "When she got on the phone, I commended her for her warm words and sentiments and shared that I was so sorry for her loss."

Michelle also asked the woman to count on her for emotional and spiritual help, and anything else she needed. Michelle told her, "Lean on me" when and if she needed anything, in whatever way Michelle could offer comfort or direction. She told me that the woman's words over the phone have stayed with her throughout the years. "What she shared with me has followed me all the days of my life with my husband."

The young expectant widow said, "Mrs. Nash, I wanted to tell you that you are married to a remarkable soldier. My husband, P.J., never met your husband, but to receive a personal check in the mail from a fellow soldier—one who never met our family—has touched my heart, and I know my husband's looking out for him and his needs even though he is no longer with us!" The woman continued, "Your soldier of a husband also said not to plan on paying you back, that we would need it more than you ever would." There was more. "Mrs. Nash, if the Army never commends your husband for this selfless act, know that my family has!" Michelle felt speechless, humbled, and blessed beyond measure, but her heart was breaking for the young woman as she was also proud of her husband. "I hung up the phone and cried and seriously thought: I am married to a hero!"

They all stayed in touch for many years after that fateful loss in Korea. Michelle recalled, "A family who I never met personally has impacted my life for over twenty-three years!"

By Dawn's Early Light

Grateful Hearts

Despite all of the pain, uncertainty, suffering, loss, and sacrifice that goes with military life, there comes a healthy pride and swelling heart over the commitment and heroism of our soldiers. Army wife Diane Joyce Bridon said, "I am honored to be a military wife. It is a noble career. My husband loves serving our country, which gives me great peace." She said she is thankful for the great friendships that she has made throughout their moves. As difficult as the moves are and will continue to be, Diane and so many others have grown in their faith, have learned more about the world in which they live, and have come to share their hearts with their military "soul sisters" in Christ in the Church all around the world.

Diane stated that, as part of the military family, "you can travel the world. You can help others all around the world, loving our country and defending our freedom." She said, "You can experience our Catholic Faith in a way that truly highlights how universal it is, through experiences with so many cultures, races, and locales that have vibrant, loving, on-fire Catholics!"

Military life has truly deepened Diane's faith. She said, "We did not really begin to truly learn, live, and love our Catholic Faith until six or seven years into our marriage. As we traveled, we experienced fantastically holy Army priests and faithful souls in many different places, and Dan lived through some of the difficulties of war in Iraq." Years of service strengthened them. "Seven years assigned to the U.S. Army in Europe (USAREUR) solidified our faith as we visited so many holy places, saw incorrupt saints and our Catholic historical heritage." Diane added, "We attended Mass with the pope—twice! Seeing one hundred plus nations' militaries represented by Catholics in uniform from around the world at the Fiftieth Annual Military Pilgrimage to Lourdes vividly emphasized to me and my family how universal our Catholic Church is!" All of these amazing "perks" have been a wonderful part of Diane's and so many other military women's journeys.

After twenty-six years of active duty for her husband and fifteen moves around the globe and counting, Michelle Nash also shared some heartfelt sentiments about being an Army wife. She said, "The best-ever moments truly have been in the traditional sense when I am standing at a military function with the military band playing, the Color Guard walking out on a field, standing by my husband in his uniform and hearing the National Anthem played and *knowing* it is more than just a song but a *true anthem* in my life." She further noted, "Much like our Catholic Faith, military traditions keep me grounded and appreciating what all this means and what lives it has cost, and I am forever grateful on both accounts as a military spouse and baptized daughter in the family of Christ."

Michelle loves the adventure and commitment of the military. "I am truly blessed to share what the old Army saying was, 'Not just a job but an adventure.' I would accurately say that it's my husband's job and my *adventure*! I am grateful for this way of life and all those whose journeys I have been able to share along the way. God bless our military and God bless America!" she declared jubilantly.

Matthew 10:28

Do not fear those who kill the body but cannot kill the soul; rather fear him who can destroy both soul and body in hell.

The Thirst of Jesus

When Jesus hung dying on the Cross, He uttered the words "I thirst." All around the world, in Missionaries of Charity convent chapels, the words "I thirst" are painted on the wall near the altar and the tabernacle. Mother Teresa wanted all who visited to be reminded of Jesus' thirst for our love and that we should thirst for His. Jesus said: "Let anyone who thirsts come to me and drink" (John 7:37, NABRE). As well, He told us, "Whoever drinks the water I shall give will never thirst" (John 4:14, NABRE). Jesus thirsts for our love. Let us meet Him at the "well" of prayer often to quench His thirst and ours.

The Fruit of Silence
Mother Teresa (1910–1997)

The fruit of silence is prayer.
The fruit of prayer is faith.
The fruit of faith is love.
The fruit of love is service.

Prayer for Daily Service
Mother Teresa (1910–1997)

Make us worthy, Lord,
to serve our fellow men

Express Gratitude

throughout the world
who live and die
in poverty and hunger.

Give them through our hands
this day their daily bread,
and by our understanding love,
give peace and joy. Amen.

Lord, Open Our Eyes
Mother Teresa (1910–1997)

Lord, open our eyes,
that we may see You
in our brothers and sisters.

Lord, open our ears,
that we may hear the cries
of the hungry, the cold,
the frightened, the oppressed.

Lord, open our hearts,
that we may love each other
as You love us.

Renew in us Your spirit.
Lord, free us and make us one. Amen.

The Value of a Grain of Rice and Ordinary Tasks

Sometimes the tiniest things—such as a grain of rice, a cookie crumb, or even a rotten pear—can make a huge impact on our hearts and souls. Are they really tiny, after all? I'll never forget volunteering in the Missionaries of Charity soup kitchen in Harlem, New York, back when it was very dangerous in Harlem. The streets were lined with abandoned, stripped-down vehicles and barbed wire seemed to be the decoration of choice. The loving sisters of Mother Teresa worked miracles using someone else's donated leftovers and discarded foods to create feasts for the hungry who came in droves to eat at their soup kitchen. I was invited by Servant of God Fr. John Hardon, S.J., my former spiritual director, to partake in a long weekend of prayer and volunteering with the sisters at the convent when he would be there to give the sisters an Ignatian retreat. That weekend, Mother Teresa was there, too.

The only caveat, if we can call it that, was that I'd be sleeping on a somewhat rickety bunk bed in the women's shelter alongside women from all sorts of backgrounds. I managed to survive the mostly sleepless nights and dove in to participating alongside the sisters during their times in the chapel. I rolled up my sleeves to help whenever I could, especially in serving the poor at their soup kitchen—piling the food high on the plates because it might be their only meal that day. Every once in a while, a glance would pierce my heart as the eyes of the guests caught mine when I handed their plate of food over the counter to them. Words can't express those encounters. I surely began to understand Mother Teresa's description of God's poor when she spoke of "Jesus in the distressing disguise of the poorest of the poor." I learned so much from Mother Teresa, the sisters, and the guests during that precious time in Harlem.

Express Gratitude

Something powerful struck me to the core when a Missionaries of Charity sister reached into the trash can, where I had just tossed a rotten pear, and bringing it back to me, she pointed to the one salvageable part that could be cut off and used in the fruit salad that we were making to serve later that evening. Every little bit would help to create a feast for the poor. That has stayed with me; it is etched on my heart.

Another time, my family shared a meal with Fr. Hardon at a McDonald's restaurant. Because of his vow of poverty, Father didn't eat at fancy restaurants. After the meal, he looked down at a few stray French fries that my little daughter Jessica had left behind on her tray. He asked, "What would Mother Teresa think?" Wow, what a conviction! Mother Teresa would never waste a thing.

When Mother Teresa once brought a dish of rice to a poor family, the mother of the family thanked the petite nun and excused herself to bring half of what had been given to her to her next-door neighbors, who were hungry, too. The neighbors were of a different faith, but that didn't stop the woman from sharing with them the little that she had. Mother Teresa was impressed and thankful.

When in prison, Cardinal Francis Xavier Nguyen Van Thuan wrote:

A rich person may not think of gathering up leftover bread and fish from his or her dinner table, but a poor person knows the value of a grain of rice. For a poor person a grain of rice is like gold, and what is gathered is not for that person alone, but to have something on hand to share with others.

I must know how to gather the most ordinary tasks to myself and to accomplish them as well as possible and with all of my love. For spiritual poverty is also careful not to lose the smallest crumb. Jesus was poor and he said, "Gather up what remains."[89]

I want to mention a powerful teaching from dear Mother Teresa, who had said that it is far easier to serve a dish of rice to satisfy the hunger of someone on the other side of the world than it is to serve that dish of rice or "dish of love" to someone in our own homes. Serving that "dish of rice" on the other side of the world translates to helping in missionary work away from home, sending a check to help, and so on. Serving that "dish of love" at home means listening to the needs around you and loving with Christ's love, even when it is difficult to do so, as in the case of a troubled person or a family member feeling unloved for some reason. This could be in your family at home or in your military family. Take some time to ponder who that might be and pray that God will grant you the graces to serve that "dish of love."

Speaking of "little" things, I can still see the twinkle in my father's eyes when he was in his hospital bed eating an oatmeal-raisin cookie I had baked for him. He dropped a crumb on the bed and then scooped it up right away and put it into his mouth! He didn't want to miss a crumb! Do we "gather up what remains," as Jesus instructs? Are we careful "not to lose the smallest crumb" in our spiritual lives, as Cardinal Van Thuan mentions? Do we attempt to accomplish all of our ordinary daily tasks as well as we possibly can, or do we do them to get them over with or only half-heartedly? Let us also reflect upon the need to care for "Jesus in the distressing disguise of the poorest of

[89] Nguyễn, *Prayers of Hope, Words of Courage*, 22.

the poor," as Mother Teresa exhorts us to do. Who is that Jesus? Is He living in a family member with whom I'm having trouble, or a neighbor I should get to know? "Blessed are those who hear the word of God and observe it!" (Luke 11:28, NABRE). Let us open our ears!

To You, O Lord, I Lift Up My Soul

In this chapter, we have discussed reflecting on our lives, expressing gratitude to God, and recognizing the importance of "tiny," seemingly insignificant things—even a grain of rice, a piece of rotten fruit, or a cookie crumb. As well, I've mentioned how it is sometimes very difficult to serve our family members with a "dish of rice" or "dish of love." What could these reflections mean in your life? Could you take some time to ponder and pray—thanking God for all His amazing blessings?

With All My Love

Dear Lord, Jesus, I love You.
I want to love You even more.

With a grateful heart,
I thank You for blessing me
with the gift of my military family.

Please open my heart
and help me to be attentive
to all the needs around me,
knowing that You are counting on me
to reach out with Your love
to ease their pain
and bring light into their lives. Amen.

Acknowledgments

I want to thank Michelle Nash, president of the Military Council of Catholic Women, and Elizabeth Tomlin, former president of the MCCW, for their enthusiasm when I told them that I would write this book for military women. As well, I want to thank the courageous military women and others who have shared their personal testimonies openly for this book so that readers can be helped and inspired.

I'd like to thank heartily the Military Council of Catholic Women for the honor they bestowed upon me of "lifetime member of the MCCW." What a blessing!

I am blessed to be working with Sophia Institute Press to get this book out to you. It has been my great pleasure to work with Charlie McKinney and the wonderful staff at Sophia.

I write in remembrance of my father, Eugene Joseph Cooper, who served in the National Guard. We shared a little routine each night, in which I would run to get his slippers when he came home from work. I'd untie his work shoes and put his slippers on his tired, aching feet. I fondly recall a story about my father, who, in his attempt at humor, would often ask, "What are you doing, writing a book?" whenever one of his friends or co-workers peppered him with questions. So, I say now, "Well, yes, Daddy, your little girl is writing a book. This one is dedicated to you!"

I also write in remembrance of my big brother Gary John Cooper, who served in the Vietnam War and told a story about being stuck in a foxhole with a cobra and having to fire every bullet in his rifle at it, finally risking his life to escape to another foxhole to get away from the deadly snake! Dear brother Gary, I still have the beautiful string of pearls you gave me at Christmas when I was sixteen years old!

My big brother Timothy John Cooper also served in Vietnam. I remember vividly that when Tim was a young teenager, he used to trick me into allowing him to finish my Dairy Queen ice cream cones! I finally caught on to his clever way of getting some extra ice cream. On a more serious note, I am very proud of you, Tim, and blessed to be your little sister.

I am blessed by my family: my parents, Eugene Joseph Cooper and Alexandra Mary Uzwiak Cooper, and my brothers and sisters: Alice Jean, Gene, Gary, Barbara, Tim, Michael, and David. I love you all!

My husband, David, is the wind beneath my wings. Thank you for your love and support. I love you!

My children—Justin, Chaldea, Jessica, Joseph, and Mary-Catherine—are my greatest joy in life. My grandchildren, Shepherd James and Leo Arthur, bless me with unending joy. May God continue to bless all of you. I love you so much!

Finally, I want to thank those who accompany me along this amazing pilgrimage through life—those I meet along the way and all those who read my books, listen to my talks, or watch my television shows. Please be assured of my continual prayers for you. Kindly pray for me, too. We are all on this

Acknowledgments

journey together! Let us pray for and help one another along the way — striving, with God's amazing grace, to bring countless souls to Heaven!

Resources

Archdiocese for the Military Services, USA

www.milarch.org
Resources, news, events, and information on becoming a chaplain,
evangelization and catechesis, sacramental records, and more.

Military One Source

www.militaryonesource.mil
From the website: "To be the one source that stands ready to
assist as you master military life. To give you expert support and
information that is proven and practical. To be there, day and
night, wherever you are, when you need a trusted voice, private
and confidential. To have answers you can depend on in pursuit
of your best goals and your best MilLife. To be one dedicated
community whose sole mission is you."

Military Council of Catholic Women

http://mccw.org
From the website: "MCCW-Worldwide is recognized and
endorsed as the official women's organization within the

Archdiocese for the Military Services, USA. MCCW women support their military parish communities in ministry and collaborate with chaplains according to the Vatican II document, *Decree on Bridging of the Laity*."

National Military Family Organization

www.militaryfamily.org

From the website: "NMFA is the voice of military families because, for 48 years, we have proven that we stand behind service members, their spouses, and their children. Our Association is the 'go to' source for Administration Officials, Members of Congress, and key decision makers when they want to understand issues facing our families. They know we have 'boots on the ground' with military families and understand better than anyone that 'military families serve, too.' Through the support and programs we provide, and our respected voice on Capitol Hill, at the Pentagon, and the Veterans Administration, our Association always looks out for the families who stand behind the uniform and for those who serve."

Tragedy Assistance Program for Survivors

www.taps.org

From the website: "The Tragedy Assistance Program for Survivors (TAPS) offers compassionate care to all those grieving the loss of a military loved one. Since 1994, TAPS has provided comfort and hope 24/7 through a national peer support network and connection to grief resources, all at no cost to surviving families and loved ones."

Resources

U.S. Conference of Catholic Bishops

www.usccb.org/

From the website: "The United States Conference of Catholic Bishops (USCCB) is an assembly of the hierarchy of the United States and the U.S. Virgin Islands who jointly exercise certain pastoral functions on behalf of the Christian faithful of the United States. The purpose of the Conference is to promote the greater good which the Church offers humankind, especially through forms and programs of the apostolate fittingly adapted to the circumstances of time and place. This purpose is drawn from the universal law of the Church and applies to the episcopal conferences which are established all over the world for the same purpose."

About the Author

Mother of five and a grandmother as well, Donna-Marie Cooper O'Boyle is known to millions as the comforting voice and smiling face of Catholic womanhood. No stranger to the difficulties and great joys woven into the tapestry of motherhood, Donna-Marie was once a single mother. She knows all about the demands for perfection aimed at women and the allurements of our darkened culture. She aims to help Catholic mothers, women, and families navigate their sublime yet challenging vocation by encouraging them, reminding them of their God-given dignity, and equipping them with the necessary Catholic tools, prayers, and Church teachings.

A frequent guest on national and international television and radio, Donna-Marie is the EWTN host and creator of three television series for mothers and families, an international speaker, an award-winning journalist, a best-selling author of more than twenty-five books, and an honorary lifetime member of the Military Council for Catholic Women. She weaves into her work wisdom from her ten-year friendship with St. Teresa of Calcutta and spiritual direction from Fr. John Hardon, S.J. Donna-Marie was invited by the Holy See to participate in an international congress for Catholic women at the Vatican in 2008, which focused on "*Mulieris Dignitatem*: On the Dignity and Vocation of Women." St. John Paul II bestowed a special blessing on Donna-Marie for her work on Mother Teresa.

Donna-Marie resides in New England with her family, rejoicing in God's beautiful creation. Learn more about her at www.donnacooperoboyle.com and www.feedingyourfamilyssoul.com.

Sophia Institute

Sophia Institute is a nonprofit institution that seeks to nurture the spiritual, moral, and cultural life of souls and to spread the Gospel of Christ in conformity with the authentic teachings of the Roman Catholic Church.

Sophia Institute Press fulfills this mission by offering translations, reprints, and new publications that afford readers a rich source of the enduring wisdom of mankind.

Sophia Institute also operates two popular online Catholic resources: CrisisMagazine.com and CatholicExchange.com.

Crisis Magazine provides insightful cultural analysis that arms readers with the arguments necessary for navigating the ideological and theological minefields of the day. *Catholic Exchange* provides world news from a Catholic perspective as well as daily devotionals and articles that will help you to grow in holiness and live a life consistent with the teachings of the Church.

In 2013, Sophia Institute launched Sophia Institute for Teachers to renew and rebuild Catholic culture through service to Catholic education. With the goal of nurturing the spiritual, moral, and cultural life of souls, and an abiding respect for the role and work of teachers, we strive to provide materials and programs that are at once enlightening to the mind and ennobling to the heart; faithful and complete, as well as useful and practical.

Sophia Institute gratefully recognizes the Solidarity Association for preserving and encouraging the growth of our apostolate over the course of many years. Without their generous and timely support, this book would not be in your hands.

www.SophiaInstitute.com
www.CatholicExchange.com
www.CrisisMagazine.com
www.SophiaInstituteforTeachers.org

Sophia Institute Press® is a registered trademark of Sophia Institute.
Sophia Institute is a tax-exempt institution as defined by the
Internal Revenue Code, Section 501(c)(3). Tax I.D. 22-2548708.